IRAQ, THEIR MISSION, OUR JOURNEY

IRAQ, THEIR MISSION, OUR JOURNEY

America's Destiny

Jackie Wilson

Jackie Ruth Wilson

Iraq, Their Mission, Our Journey
America's Destiny
All Rights Reserved.
Copyright © 2011 Jackie Ruth Wilson
v3.0

Editors: Elder Melissa Busick and Evangelist Jackie Wilson
Co-editors: Michael Vollmar, George Doyle and Felicia Henry.

Scripture quotations are from the Kings James Version used by permission.
Some information in this book is unauthorized.

J.R.W., "LOGO" belongs to JackieWilsonMinistries

jrw1952@gmail.com
wilson.jackie5953@yahoo.com
http://www.cafepress.com/jrwdesigns
www.outskirtspress.com/iraqtheirmissionourjourney
My God Delivers On Time. www.createspace.com/3107362

ISBN: 978-0-578-07490-0

Library of Congress Control Number: 2011901240

PRINTED IN THE UNITED STATES OF AMERICA

Table of Contents

Preface

⌘

Iraq, Their Mission, Our Journey, a continuation of my first publication entitled, My God Delivers On Time was written to honor our deceased mother, Evangelist/ Prophetess Sarah Mae Wilson's legacy, our Heroes of a Foreign War, which includes the Ohio Army National Guard 612th Engineer Battalion and especially the Bravo Company 1st Squad 1st Platoon (The Bad Boyz). I also honor the families of our military.

I write books to remind us of God's Sovereignty in predestination and ordination, and to invite you to become members of the body of Christ. Additionally, I write books for inspiration, motivation, and encouragement. *God delivers on time.*

God has a divine plan, purpose, and destiny for Iraq. No other nation except Israel has more biblical history and prophecy associated with it than Iraq. This nation is rich in oil supplies and other nations are trying to overtake them. Names in the Bible for Iraq are Babylon, land of Shinar, and Mesopotamia. Some biblical events that transpired in Iraq were Daniel in the lion's den, Noah building the Ark, the tower of Babel, Garden of Eden, the three Hebrew children placed in the fiery furnace, and Abraham resided there. For a better understanding of Iraq's history, read and study God's Word, using the Old Testament, and cross-reference each scripture in your Bible to verify this truth. *God delivers on time.*

My belief has always been that your son should volunteer for the military to become mature men and learn to give back to his country. My former husband was in the United States Marine Corp. He has many relatives who served our country. They volunteered for the military for varies reasons. They wanted to graduate from college, buy homes, and foremost secure their families. After my son's graduation, he volunteered for the Ohio Army National Guard; however, he never dreamed of going cross-seas to war; the National Guard was to protect our country.

Following 9-11, from the oval office desk, President George W Bush informed us that weapons of mass destruction existed in Iraq that was threatening our nation's security. He announced the beginning of military operations there, and we were overwhelmed. In the meantime, many have questioned President Bush's reason for ordering our military to bomb Iraq.

"Did he abuse his authority?" "Did our Heroes of a

Foreign War bring hope of freedom to Iraq?"

I support our troop's efforts; however, I will attempt to answer these questions in my conclusion at the end of this book. *God delivers on time.*

God has a divine plan and purpose for America. Based on God's foreknowledge and His divine declaration, God chose the United States of America's destiny. His purpose was/is for us to fulfill His plan of salvation.

The year of 2005-2006 was traumatic for our family. Seven relatives including our mother went to the presence of God in Paradise. My son and godson faced the death angel while serving in Iraq. One of my daughters and her unborn child, and I faced the death angel. I was angry with God, grief stricken, and exhausted; nevertheless, I share our journey to be a blessing to others. *God delivers on time.*

I pray that you will gain knowledge from this book that will make you aware of God's presence in this world and give you a desire to make Jesus Christ Lord of your personal life. I pray that you will discover God's divine plan, purpose, and destiny, which is God's perfect will for your life. I pray that God will strengthen us through this difficult period. I also pray that our troops will return home sound in body, soul, and spirit. In the meantime, it is imperative that our faith and trust remain in God for endurance until Jesus returns. *God delivers on time.*

Acknowledgements

I would like to acknowledge God, Jesus Christ, and the Holy Spirit. Additionally, Pastor Edward and Co-Pastor Shirley Tibbs-New Life Christian Ministries, and Dr. H. Frank Taylor III - Tabernacle Missionary Baptist Church. In addition, Pastor Stanley Jordan-Prayer Garden COGIC, Pastor Kennedy Dennard Sr.-New Beginnings Ministries, Elder Fredrick D. Dunlap-Friendship Missionary Baptist, Pastor C.M. Manley-New Morning Star Missionary Baptist Church, Elder Joe Robinson-Bible Way Temple Church, Reverend Dr. Jessie C. Keaton-Memorial United Methodist Church, Pastor David Howe-Trinity United Methodist Church , and Ministers Ron and Jean Moore-The Firm Foundation Ministries.

Samuel, Isaiah, and Raymond Wilson, my brothers, Inez Rogers, my sister, Clara White, my god sister, Reather Harris Chambers, John and Bessie Hector, Mary (deceased)Williams, my cousins, Clyde Rogers Jr., and Raymond D. Wilson my nephews.

My children: Keesha Smith, Tomika Lowe, Todochi Wells, and Derek Hunker, my godson.

Furthermore Mother Readie Tibbs, Gladys Turner, Ociseleen Robinson, Georgie Dunlap, Helen Washington (deceased) Mary Denson, and Deloyce Kirkman. James Sorrell, Deacon Joseph (deceased) and Evangelist Georgia McFadden, Minister Alfred Lewis Jones I, Minister of Music, Alfred Lewis Jones II, Elders Mary and Lisa Bradley, Elder Arthur and Dorothy Knuckles, Elder Alex and Barbara Townsend, and Deaconesses LaDonna and Mya Jones.

I am also acknowledging Eugene and Ann McNeal, Johnny and Colleen Hall, Terry and Carolyn Dennard, Arthur and Arnitia Edwards, William and Eunice Haqq, Lula fields, Heather Hunker, Claire Hunker, Heather Mellott, Roseanne (Roxie) Johnson, James Grizzle, Sheila Hunt, Anna Andersson, Lola Gomez, Lynn Clark, Florence (Diane) Simpson, Maggie Simpson, Willie Russell Williams, Emma McNeal, Bonnie Morgan, Theresa Henry, Kathleen Amerson, Maxine Hubbard, Stephanie Dennard, Theresa Skupsky, Brian Pitts, Jerry Morgan, Deborah (Debbie) Hall, Diane Kuipers, and Telesha R. Gibson.

St. Rita's Medical Center Emergency Room Staff, Dr. Bell, Chaplin Tom Niese, and my angel nurses. Hanna's Family Practice-Dr. Hanna and Dr. Verma, Lima Pulmo-

ACKNOWLEDGEMENTS

nary and Critical Care Association Inc, Sleep Clinic of Lima Staff Dr Kuchipudi, The Heart Institute Dr. Arabpour, Gerad Center for Cancer Treatment-Dr. Amer, Gastro-Internal Medicine-Dr. Leifer, and Eye Surgeons & Consultants Pajka Eye Clinic-Doctors and Staff: Allen County Council On Aging Inc-Executive Director Diane J. Bishop, Elderly Daycare Center Program Co-ordinator Lorain K. Lovett, PSA 3 Agency On Aging, (Passport Staff) Special Home Aides Joyce Williams and Jenera Knuckles. Divine Home Care Of Ohio LLC, P&R Medical Supplies, Adaptive Medical Concepts Inc, Mitchell Home Medical Inc, Bravo Company 612th Military Staff, the Red Cross, Major Amerson, professional photographer, Jones/Clark Funeral Home, Inc, and the others too numerous to mention.

Our family thanks you for your prayers and support during the most traumatic journey in our lives. *God delivers on time.*

CITY OF LIMA, OHIO

David J. Berger, Major
50 Town Square
Lima, Ohio 45801- 4900
419/228-5462
Fax 419/221-5214
www.cityhall.lima.oh.us

January 2009

Dear Reader,

When Jackie Wilson first appeared in my office several years ago to share her story, it was not possible to ignore her energy and drive. Nor was it possible to discount the internal spiritual journey that she had trod.

Jackie's first book-My God Delivers On Time-was therefore born from an inner voice that sought to describe her personal individual journey for all that would care to listen and learn.

With Jackie's second book-Iraq, Their Mission, Our Journey-she had reached spiritual insights while focused outside of herself. Her vision is now global and her inner voice speaks to issues and concerns that are inter-personal and political.

The passion of her writing endows it with energy that the reader will appreciate.

Sincerely,

David J. Berger

David J. Berger, Mayor of Lima, Ohio

ENDORSEMENTS

This is intended for all the brave women and men of the mighty 612th Engineer Battalion and especially for the Bravo Company 1st Squad 1st Platoon, "The Bad Boyz." We started out on a journey of unknown in a foreign land with people trying to do bad things to anyone who stood for the good.

During our 14 months of long deployment, there were many highs and lows. We, as Army National Guards out of Ohio set many standards and records for all to follow. Thanks to those who shed their blood, sweat, and tears including myself. It was a true honor to serve with this platoon. I hope the 612th Engineering Battalion, "Tried and Proven" made a difference in Iraq. I know the, "The Bad Boyz" made some noise, and the Barbarians were proud to have us in their country.

To my soldiers, you know that I appreciate your hard work, and I am very proud of you. To my fallen comrade Sergeant Jeremy Hodge, I thank you for allowing me to be your leader and for your ultimate sacrifice. I Salute You! You are gone, but not forgotten.

I thank Ms. Wilson for a wonderful tribute in honoring our Heroes of a Foreign War, which includes her son, Sergeant Todochi A. Wells. God's speed and blessings to all, and please continue to support the troop!

Garland L. Paynthar

Garland L. Paynthar

First Sergeant
Ohio Army National Guard

IRAQ, THEIR MISSION, OUR JOURNEY

Let me first start by thanking Mama J. (the authoress) who has always been there to offer her support. I was in Iraq for two months before being critically injured. It was one of the most influential times in my life, and I would not change a single thing.

I chose to protect this great nation, so others I love would not have to. There is no greater satisfaction in life than knowing that you are helping strangers sleep peacefully at night. There is no warmer feeling than seeing small children from another country smiling and yelling "U.S.A" as you drove past them in armored vehicles.

Serving in Iraq made me truly appreciate how wonderful life and our nation are. Protecting this country is the greatest honor a person can have. I thank God for placing me in the position to guard our borders daily while helping to spread God's Word.

I want to thank all veterans who served or are serving in the military. My time was just another link in the chain of protection. God bless the United States of America.

Sergeant Derek Hunker
Sergeant Derek Hunker

Honoring Heroes of a Foreign War

Bravo Company 612ᵗʰ Engineer Battalion

Garland Paynthar, Dustyn Antoine, Eric Allen Ardner, Keith Kenneth Arnold, Ricardo Arreguin, Jason Baldwin, Jeffrey Lynn Beckley Jr., John Beeler, Jeffrey Todd Berling, Nicole Susann Bertschy, Andrew Blackburn, Brian Bolander, Gerald Bond, Jon Boucher, Gregory Broseus, Timothy Brown, and Erick Browning. Darin Burton, Thomas Butler, Scott Camera, William Campbell, Ashley Carrier, Manuel Castillo, Andrew Charles, *Jeremy Chase*, Paolo Cici, David Cobb, Scott Cole, William Cousins, Bryan Crandall, Jess Daniels, Patrick Dehnart, and George Dewalt.

Jordan Diller, Joshua Dooley, Sean Druckenmiller, Bruce Esparza, Andrew Flechtner, Brandon Frier, Justin Gastony, Keith Gault, *Vincant Gillfillan*, Jeffrey Gillmore, Nicholas Lynn Gochenauer, Joseph Gurney, Jerad Hanefeld, Jeffrey Hansis, and Kevin Hauenstein. Michael Gene Hay, George

Henderson, *Jeremy Hodge* * killed in action (KIA) * Edward Holt, Jay Hossler, John Hrivnak, *Derek Hunker* (godson), Donald Jacobs, Nicholas Johnson, *Paul Tricket*, Sheldon Johnson, Kevin Kaiser, Jonathan Karpus, Izzet Kessler, Kyle Knoblock, Keith Kolasinski, and William Krese.

Douglas Laile, Bryan Lieb, Darren Linthicum, Samuel Livingston, Russell Lott, Jamin Lozano, Jared Donald Martin, Richard McMeechan, Mcrae Meade, James Mesley, *Nathanial Mellott*, Keith Michael Melvin, Christian Michael, Allen Minton, and Andrew Molter. Mark Molyet, Jason Moore, Eric Mussinan, *Jarrod Nighswander*, Michael Peters, Michael Pflieger, Samuel Ortiz, Robert Penwell, Jason Powell, John Pradelski, Joshua Priddy, Seth Pugh, Richard Randolph and Brian Regovich. Jonathon Rice, Juan Riveramartinez, Robert Roach, Matthew Roush, Russell Stanton, Jose Salcedo, Ernest Sampson, Kevin Scarpino, Brandon Scurlock, Andrew Showalter, Jerime Shuck, Jason Sindel, Ronald Smith, and Brandon Springer. Alex Straub, Theresa A. Szczerban, Benjamin Taylor, Thomas Vogan, Jeremiah Weiker, Derek Welch*, Todochi Wells* (son), Darin White, Joshua Wilson, and Roy Young.

Older men start wars; young men fight wars. The Bravo Company 1st Squad 1st Platoon (The Bad Boyz) has been *"Tried and Proven."* God has given our Heroes of a Foreign War a destiny including, Paul N. Busick, and other too numerous to mention. *God delivers on time.*

1

America Bombed Iraq

Following 9-11, America bombed Iraq, and we were overwhelmed. Our troops had embarked on a journey of the unknown in a foreign land. People were killing anyone who represented good. A war to disarm a state became a fight against insurgency. Terrorism and sectarian warfare was tarring Iraq apart. The military had not properly trained our troops in disarming Improvised Explosive Device (I.E.D) roadside bombs; therefore, they were dying daily and others were injured. Yet, at every turn, our troops were serving with courage and resolve. They were determined to complete every mission given including defeat a regime that was terrorizing the Iraqi people. In the meantime, our relations aboard were strained and unity at home was being tested. The media had no positive news to report to us about Iraq. Violence was escalating daily. *God delivers on time.*

My son Todochi had graduated from Lima Senior High School and was attending Tiffin University in Tiffin, Ohio, concentrating in Business Administration. He joined the Army National Guard in Tiffin shortly after his first semester in December 2000. Prior to him becoming a soldier, he was active in extracurricular activities and volunteer organizations. He touched many lives through relief effects and by providing domestic security. He has also served as a role model for his peers and others. His high level of commitment to community involvement and helping others played a major role in his decision to join the Army National Guard. He never dreamed that the National Guard would go cross-seas to fight, but remain here and protect America. The war in Iraq remained on his mind. In the meantime, I kept praying and hoping that the military would not deploy him there.

In 2003, I decided to give our mother Ms. Sarah Wilson a special (80th) birthday celebration in Lima, Ohio that would affect her life and ours forever. God had blessed her with many gifts and talents. She recognized God's voice, so I asked God not to reveal to her our plans for her birthday celebration. He answered our prayers. Thanks to our pastor Dr. H. Frank Taylor III, she thought that our church was having a picnic. In the meantime, I contacted my only brother-in-law Clyde Rogers Sr, and my sister Inez, and they secured Lima's Faurot largest pavilion for this great event. He always had my back. When I was 6 years old, Mother's fear prevented her from buying me a bike, so he purchased one for me. Mother and I have similar voice tones; therefore, there were times when he did not recognize that it was I talking with him.

I contacted my oldest brother Samuel Wilson. He and his wife Sylvia and their family agreed to participate. There were times when he could not recognize my voice either. I had fun when he called our mother's home. He always mentioned that I sound just like our mom. Then, he would tell me to get off the telephone. We laughed. I called my second oldest brother Isaiah. He and his wife Carolynn agreed to participate. My brother Raymond and his friend Cheryl agreed to participate. My nephew Clyde Jr., agreed to participate. E-mails and letters went out to others and everyone agreed to participate. Hotel rooms were reserved. T-shirts and a cake were designed with Mother's picture and text stating, "Happy 80th Birthday Mother Sarah Wilson." Our church family and I were to provide the food. I hired Major Amerson, our professional photographer.

Clyde and Inez arrived early to assist me with the final preparations on August 18. While we were shopping, Mother called my cell phone complaining about having feet issues. Our secret of them being in town was about to be revealed. After we arrived at Mother's apartment, she was shocked and excited about seeing her daughter and son-in-law there. I drove her to our doctor anyway, but she was fine. The enemy then tried to spoil her celebration by burning the ribs up, but thank God for our pastor Dr.

Taylor and Pastor C. M. Manley for saving the day. *God delivers on time.*

The day of Mother's birthday celebration, Todochi came home from college, and we were happy to see him. He made a decision to get Mother's beautiful designer birthday cake from the store for me, and I was grateful. I later drove to Mother's apartment, styled her hair, and presented the designer t-shirt to her. She was grateful because no one had ever designed a t-shirt for her before. Afterward, I drove her to the Faurot Park. She was shocked at seeing Samuel, Isaiah, Raymond and their families, and many others there. At that moment, she was temporarily speechless, but still without a clue that this was her birthday celebration. Finally, Mother saw her sister Louise, (who had been diagnosed with cancer) and her daughter Reather were there, and she was flabbergasted.

"Look what God has done. Here is my sister, ya'll. Oh my Lord. Lord have mercy. Look what God has done," she finally cried.

I noticed tears running down auntie's face as they embraced. Inez and I were also crying. Then, Todochi arrived carrying her beautiful birthday cake. He noticed the shocked of Mother seeing her children and sister there on her face. She then noticed her designer cake and t-shirt, and she was astounded. Inez had to calm her down. She was afraid that because of all the excitement Mother would have a heart attack. Suddenly, we started to sing, "Happy Birthday" to her.

"Jackie Ruth, how did you pull this off, girl? Lord, have mercy. Look what God has done!" she cried.

We finally ate, fellowshipped, and had a joyous time. We later drove to Mother's apartment to finish the celebration. There, she received many gifts, cards including funds.

The following day, God used Mother to pray, prophesy, and testify to us. She thanked God for His many blessings and asked Him to continue to bless us. Our families then returned to their homes, and I to bed. There were four generations of our family that attended Mother's birthday celebration. This was the first time anyone had given her a birthday festivity of this magnitude. She talked about her surprise birthday celebration for years. We sacrificed for our mother's birthday celebration. This event was costly, time consuming and exhausting; nevertheless, we did not mind. She was our mother, and we loved her. Love is an action word. We did not talk about loving her, but showed her how much we cared. *God delivers on time.*

Education was essential to Mother. She knew education was security and freedom. She believed in setting goals. She instilled into us that prayer, hard work, patience, determination, remaining focused and striving for the best would enable us to achieve our goals. Most importantly, do your best and God will do the rest. *God delivers on time.*

Mother faced many adversities; nevertheless, she never gave up. She was assertive. She enrolled in Thomson High School online classes at age 80. She also enrolled at the Senior Citizen Services and Elderly Daycare Center to interact with others her age. We named these Centers her "schools." One evening while visiting with her, I discovered that she had secretly enrolled in a basic computer class at the Senior Citizen Services. She placed her hand on her hip, proudly flaunting a Satisfactory Certificate of Completion for that course in my face. She was praising God for her achievement. I was shocked and excited. I tried convincing her that I would no longer assist her in getting a high school diploma, since she was so accomplished. We burst out with laughter. She knew that I was teasing and would always be there for her. She later purchased a computer and registered to go online. She sent her first e-mail to me. She typed her name, address, telephone number, and that she loved me. I saved her e-mail on a CD, which I will keep eternally.

Sometimes, Mother went to school from my home. Prior to her leaving, she always modeled what she was wearing for my approval. If I disapproved, I was no longer her designer, but her daughter. I definitely was not her mama. Following her tirade, she would relent and redress. Then, she would ask me to pack her lunch, which made me feel special. I would stand by the front door, so she could take her lunch bag and leave. She always left from my home dressed nice and smelling good. It is amazing that as our parent's age, our roles change. Before leaving, she always said, "Jackie, see you this evening when I get home. I love you."

Mother enjoyed her visits at the Senior Citizen Services and the Elderly Daycare Center. She had nice things to say and looked forward to returning there. At one point, we discussed my teaching her how to swim, but situations occurred that would not permit this. In the meantime, being gone two days a week at each center was becoming tiresome for her, so she prayed. God directed her to remain at the Elderly Daycare Center because He had a work for her to do there. She made a great impact in the lives of many people at the Senior Citizen Center.

God had highly favored and blessed Mother to achieve her goal on July 30, 2004. She graduated at age 80, received her high school diploma, and class ring. She also received a Preliminary Certificate from the Commonwealth of Pennsylvania Department of Education. Todochi also graduated from Tiffin University, receiving a Bachelor Degree in Business Administration in 2004. Marathon Petroleum, a Fortune 500 company located in Findlay, Ohio employed him. We were excited that God had answered prayer. *God delivers on time.*

Mother 81st birthday was approaching on August 19, 2004. I begin preparing a surprise celebration for her at our church. I had a designer cake created for her B-day. I also bought party favors to decorate our church. She had no clue of what I had planned for her birthday. After we arrived at the church, she was shocked at seeing Todochi, his friend Anna Andersson and many others there to celebrate her day. The Spirit of God was in the house, so we had church service. Mother and the saints danced for the Lord. Todochi and others dedicated a song to her. Everyone had nice things to say about Mother Wilson. The saints cooked the greatest food, and we served mom. Later, we sang happy birthday to her. She was excited, but she managed to blow her candles out. She received many gifts, cards including funds. We took pictures and Todochi video recorded this great event. *God delivers on time.*

The war in Iraq remained on our minds. Later, our worst fears transpired. Todochi informed me that the military deployed his unit, the Bravo Company 612th Engineer Battalion to Iraq. He then left for the shopping mall, leaving me alone to collect my thoughts. I called Mother, and she prayed for me. I called Brother Arthur and Sister Dorothy Knuckles, and he prayed. He quoted scriptures of God's promises for our heirs. He also reminded me of God's capability to protect and bring his godson (Boomer, he calls him) home whole. I later informed my daughters Keesha and Tomika of their only brother's deployment; however, at that time, they did not comment. I later researched for ways to prevent him from going there. Initially, an only son cannot be draft into the military. If he volunteers and war transpires, they could deploy him. He could possibly serve in a non-combat zone. Additionally, he could file a conscientious objector form due to his religious beliefs. To confirm this information, contact your local Veteran Administration office.

Todochi, a United States soldier would not desert a fellow soldier. He understands the importance of freedom for all people. Knowing what his options were, he chose to serve his country. He was committed to whatever task he might encounter.

"Rest assured, however, my follow soldiers and I will carry out that mission with honor, bravery and integrity," he said.

I supported his efforts, although, I opposed his decision to go to Iraq. In the meantime, I thank God for the encouragement and prayers of the saints. God gave me the strength to accept what I could not change. I activated my faith by continuing to meditate on God's Word. *God delivers on time.*

Marathon transferred Todochi to work for them in Atlanta, Georgia; however, they allowed him to return home and work, while preparing to go to Iraq. It was nice having him with us. I appreciate his employer for that. I did not know if he would be home for the holiday seasons, so we celebrated Thanksgiving Day on October 30. Our dinner menu consisted of turkey, dressing and gilbert gravy, collard greens, corn bread, potato salad, macaroni and cheese. We also had Swedish meatballs, ham casserole, cheesecakes, apple pie, and ice cream. Believing God would protect and see him home safely, I had a special cake decorated for him that stated, "Welcome Home Boober." The food was delicious. Am I making you hungry? I should be sorry, but...

Mother asked God to bless our family as well as the

food. Todochi announced his engagement to Anna, and we welcomed her to our family. We conversed about his journey to Iraq and everyone had positive thoughts about his safe return home.

Todochi reported to the Army National Guard Base on November 10. He was tardy; therefore, to prevent further tardiness, a hotel room was provided for him. Later, he sent a text message telling me what to do for him. I was no longer his Mother, but an errand girl. The Army National Guard presented him with a, "Creed of the Non-commissioned Officers Leader of Soldier's Certificate" on November 11. We will always cherish his certificate.

The Bravo Company 612th Engineer Battalion held their send-off ceremony at Heidelberg College on November 12. Veterans conducted the service, which included a song, prayer and various speakers. Meanwhile, Keesha took pictures. All involved were overwhelmed with emotions, including Todochi. My heart felt as if it would burst out of my chest. I was speechless, placed my head on his chest, and unexpectedly tears wrapped my cheeks. A concerned person approached me, wiped my face, and then she walked away. I later asked Todochi, "Who was the lady that wiped my face?"

"Sergeant Derek Hunker's mother," he replied.

After she and I officially met, it was as if we had known each other all of our lives. She had known my son since he had volunteered for the Army National Guard. Todochi and Derek have a brotherly friendship, so I adopted Derek as my godson. His mother and I decided to stay in contact with each other. Later, the military staff allowed Todochi an overnight stay with us in Lima, Ohio. We ate at the Golden Corral Restaurant, where the food was excellent, and then we returned home. He and I talked until 2:30: am about our relationship. Later that morning, my son-in-law Charles, Keesha, and I drove him to begin his journey. At one point, I could no longer hold my tears back, so I went to the restroom. Then another soldier's family member walked in, and we cried on each other's shoulders. The Holy Spirit empowered me, and I took authority. I declared that God was in control. The saints were praying for our troops nationwide. We had to trust God for their protection and a safe return home. He would console us throughout this difficult period and everything was gonna to be alright. *God delivers on time.*

We left from the restroom, rejoined our troops, and many pictures were taken. In the meantime, a concerned individual approached me wanting to know Todochi's military occupational specialty (MOS). At that time, I did not know, so I asked him.

"I am a Combat Engineer," he proudly replied.

His answer did not console my nervous system or my psychological status. I forgot that *God delive*red *on time.* I was temporarily insane.

"Boy, what were you thinking about to chose such an occupation. Were you crazy or something? Lord have mercy Jesus; help us Lord. My child has lost his mind," I cried.

"Oh mom, everything is gonna be alright, stop worrying," he calmly said.

Todochi and Derek's journey to Iraq was becoming more apparent. Before the Bravo's departure, the military staff gave us additional information. They would properly train them in the United States to defeat a regime that was terrorring the Iraqi people. Afterward, they would commute to Kuwait and then Bagdad, Iraq. Later, three buses and semi trucks arrived to transport our troops, equipment, food, and whatever else for their mission to Iraq. We embraced them and said a temporary good-bye. My human side resurfaced. My baby, a Combat Engineer was going to war. The danger he was facing had become a reality. Tears ran profusely down my cheeks. Keesha remained calm, but tears were in Charles eyes. The Holy Spirit comforted and strengthened us to move forward. Then, we drove to the mall and shopped, which helped. Later, we returned to Lima.

America had bombed Iraq. Ohio Army National Guard Bravo Company 612th Engineer Battalion, which included Todochi and Derek were to assist other troops for one year in bringing democracy to Iraq. I prayed that God would continue to provide protection for our troops and strengthen us. Our journey continues, but *God delivers on time.*

2

The Holiday Seasons

The holiday seasons were approaching; yet our journey continued. When Mother resided in Lima, she always spent Thanksgivings, Christmas, and welcomed in the New Year with me. She notified her other children; therefore, they could call her at my home. At one time, I cooked large dinners for the family, but not anymore. Keesha and Tomika cook at their residence. When Todochi is home, he eats everywhere. Sometimes we socialize at a designated location, and we have lots of fun. I was wondering what my son would be eating for Thanksgiving dinner. I drove to Keesha's house to complain, but everyone was acting bizarrely. They were distant and showed no interest in my concerns. I drove home and prepared to go to bed. Mother noticed my depressive state and tried to comfort me. I suddenly heard a knock on my back door and wondered who was there at this late hour. I opened the door and

Keesha said, "Mom, someone is here to see you."

Todochi walked in, and we embraced and cried. Then, the telephone rang. It was Sakeyna, my oldest granddaughter.

"What are you doing grandma?"

"Nothing Keyna, but did you know Boober was coming home for Thanksgiving?"

"Yes," she replied with much laughter.

I finally realized everyone knew that he was coming home except Mother and me. Todochi and I went grocery shopping at Clyde Evans (yes, at that late hour.) I later cooked; nevertheless, we ate at Keesha's home. Now, it felt like Thanksgiving because it ended up being a joyous day. *God delivers on time.*

Todochi was home for four days, and we had a great time. He did not know if he would be home for Christmas, so he went shopping for everyone. The following Sunday, Keesha and I drove him to the Army Base, returned home, and waited to hear from him. During their training period, there was no daily communication. I began to miss him greatly. Finally, he contacted me with great news. He was coming home for Christmas; however, this time, he wanted to surprise his sisters and their families. I told Mother, and she was excited. She promised not to tell anyone. Occasionally, my girls and their children asked if he was coming home for Christmas; however, I kept my promise.

Mother and I went Christmas shopping, ate out, and

had lots of fun. Later, SaKeyna, my other granddaughters including TaQuayla, Amarous and Diamond came to my home to decorate the Christmas tree and wrap presents. Mom enjoyed her great-grandchildren, and they enjoyed granny. Later, Lima had a snowstorm that gave us that look of Christmas. Then, I received a present in a large box from Todochi's employer Marathon Petroleum, and I was excited.

Todochi arrived late at night on December 23, 2004. I was sleepy but happy to have him home. Initially, he wanted to open my gift from Marathon, but I refused. This gift did not belong to him. Then, he attempted to manipulate me by saying he already knew what was in the box. God gave me the strength to refuse him again. He also begged for my collard greens that I had cooked earlier. He sounded like a one-year-old kid whining for a bottle. At that moment, he was my baby and not a soldier, so I gave in. I told him to eat the entire pot of greens if he desired, even if it meant cooking another one. He was home, and I wanted him to enjoy himself.

The following day, he dug out of our driveway, which took him about five hours. He then drove to Keesha's house and surprised them. Later, Tomika and her family joined us and were surprised as well. She and I went shopping; we had a glorious time. Our family celebrated Christmas at my home on December 25, 2004. We opened presents, ate, took many pictures, and had a joyous time. Mother enjoyed her grandchildren, great-grand children and me. Although we were enjoying ourselves, at times I felt sad and lonely. God was warning me that this would be Mother's last Christmas with us. I mentioned this to Tomika, but she did not comment. Anyway, God blessed us to celebrate Jesus birthday. Todochi was home for four days, and we had a great time. I thank Marathon for the gift of honoring our troops.

We thought Todochi would be in Iraq for the holiday seasons. Miraculously, he was home for both holidays. Keesha nominated me to drive him back to the Army Base at the end of his leave. Our journey continues, but *God delivers on time.*

3

The Transition

The transition was becoming difficult for us. From time to time, the media reported disturbing news about the war in Iraq, but God gave me the strength. My faith was not predicated on the conditions at hand. My faith was grounded in God's Word. In the meantime, I had to trust God that Todochi, Derek and others were alright. *God delivers on time*

I accompanied Mother to Pittsburgh, Pennsylvania to visit her sister, Aunt Louise on December 31, 2004. Since their mother, Mrs. Amanda Littlejohn Branan-Borders home going 34 years ago, they developed a stronger bond. They spoke weekly over the telephone. Auntie's daughter Reather was exhausted, but God had ordained and strengthened her to care for her mom. We gave them space because auntie's time on earth was expiring. I believe they had a private hardy party. While visiting, Mother had a mini stroke (transient ischemic attack TIA) and was taken by ambulance to the hospital, but later discharged. My blood pressure was high. Considering the circumstances, we had a pleasant visit. We took pictures, laughed, and ate. While we were there, Keesha called to inform us that Todochi would be calling her at home with information about his deployment. Mother and I later returned home to Lima in the midst of an ice storm.

"Mom, I love you. I am going to Iraq, and I will return home. Pray for me every day," he cried over the telephone. I also cried.

Mother remained at my home until the weather permitted her to return to hers. She slept in my bed, while I slept on the couch. Suddenly, God told me to go lay next to her. I noticed that she periodically stopped breathing in her sleep. I awakened her several times because of her breathing inconsistencies. In the meantime, she wanted me to stop interfering with her sleep. I had no idea that my life was about to change forever. I later was able to drive her to our family doctor. She examined mom and referred her to the sleep clinic for an evaluation. He diagnosed her with obstructive sleep apnea, and prescribed a Cpap machine that included a mask with nightly medication. I was uncomfortable with her living alone while using that breathing equipment, so I made a decision to become her caregiver. I also promised myself not to place her in a nursing home facility unless it was extremely necessary. At that time, I did not know God had already ordained me to care for our mother until He called her home. Additionally, I was to ensure that her home going plans happen. She remained at my home until we located a larger place to live. In the meantime, Reather and Raymond helped me to keep my promise. *God delivers on time.*

Marcus and Tomika were expecting a baby girl. We thought her pregnancy test results were incorrect. She always had boys and Keesha, girls. Her pregnancy was difficult because the doctor diagnosed her with toxemia, a deadly illness. He hospitalized her many times. Mother prayed, prophesied, and we trusted God.

Todochi contacted Keesha and me sounding exhausted and ill on January 9, 2005. As if the danger was not enough, the climate change had created health issues for him. His doctor diagnosed him with an upper respiratory infection and prescribed antibiotics. Time would only permit us to talk for a few minutes; however, it was nice hearing his voice.

Iraq's first election occurred and numerous Iraqis showed up to vote on January 30. Our military assisted them by assuring their safety; therefore, the election went well. During this time, I experienced migraine headaches. Mother suggested that I visit our family doctor, and I agreed. I discovered that my blood pressure had increased from my normal of 110/70 to 161/107. She expressed concerns and administered medication. She would not allow me to leave from her office until my blood pressure had stabilized. Todochi had always sensed when something was wrong with me. The following day, he called. I mentioned that my blood pressure was high, but it had stabilized. We thanked God.

The Bad Boyz (their war on terror name) was hit with an Improvised Explosive Device (I.E.D) roadside bomb on February 28. Sergeant Derek Hunker sustained serious head injuries, and his medical status was critical. Todochi and other troops were highly upset over Derek's injuries; however, we thanked God for His intervention. Previously, Todochi and Derek prayed, studied God's Word, and lifted weights daily. Being bunkmates, they were always concerned about each other. In the meantime, Derek was recuperating at home, and we were expecting a full recovery. Having God, excellent trained personnel, the best goggles, helmets, other protective battle gear, and good medical equipment is what saved Sergeant Hunker's life. God has a plan, purpose, and destiny for him.

Todochi's responsibilities had greatly increased. He was concerned about having the life of many in his hands. Our troops were at risk daily; however, they were committed to the mission. I commend Staff Sergeant Garland Paynthar and other troops for making a difference in Iraq. *God delivers on time.*

Todochi came home on leave for a two-week vacation on March 8. We were extremely happy to see him. He unwound for a few hours, and then he went visiting. He shopped daily. He had not spent much time with Mother or me; therefore, I took his behavior personally. God used

Mother to speak words, which brought clarity to my mind. Initially, his mental state was still in the war mode. Additionally, he could not leave the Bravo mentally in Iraq. Then, I understood. After his vacation had ended, he returned there. He called us sounding stressed, but we kept him in prayer.

One evening Mother was walking down our hallway having difficulty breathing. At this time, our family doctor was on maternity leave, so another doctor saw her. After many tests, he later diagnosed her with a cystic liver and a thoracic aneurysm, and I was shocked. God strengthen me to drive us home. Afterward, I informed my siblings, and they were saddened. I faxed and e-mailed her medical report results to Samuel and Isaiah, so they could get second opinions from their doctors. I called other family members to inform them about her medical conditions. I also released my frustration to Arnitia, Dorothy, Lola, Roseanne (Roxie) and others. They knew my plate was full because Todochi was serving in Iraq and Tomika and her unborn child was constantly facing death. I was Mother's caregiver, and I was not in the best of health; nevertheless, they always encouraged me. God strengthened me to move forward in what He had ordained me to do, which was to carry out His plan and purpose for our mother. *God delivers on time.*

One Saturday morning, Mother and I had similar dreams of us moving in a three-bedroom brick house. We moved in our home on March 27. This transitional process was difficult for us, to say the least. We were both controlling individuals. I was overprotective; however, we adjusted to our new living arrangement. I contacted PSA 3, Council On Aging and other agencies for assistance. Mother was eligible for many benefits including home care. Many aides cared for her, but I was displeased with their cleaning abilities. Finally, we accepted Jenera Knuckles as her aide, which made us happy. We had known her before adolescence. They talked a lot and developed a special bond. She loved Mother Wilson and vice versa.

One day I asked Mother's goddaughter Sister Clara White to sit with mom while I took care of business. While I was gone, our kitchen stove burned out and for months, we were without one. My godson Derek Hunker purchased a stove for us and delivered it to our home. In the meantime, God would not allow furthering bonding between Mother and Sister Clara. *God delivers on time.*

Reather often reminded me to take a break from the situation. Caring for a sick person was not an easy job, and she did not want me to become ill. I later agreed to visit my sister Elizabeth Monford in Cincinnati, Ohio. Her daughter Beverly, (who resides in Pittsburgh, Pennsylvania) and I went there together. While I was gone, SaKeyna stayed with Mother. I called home several times, and they were having a blessed quality weekend. She was taking great care of mom. She had braided her hair et cetera. After our return to Lima, Beverly went back home. She later called to inform me that Elizabeth had a mini stroke, and I was saddened. I could not visit her because of Mother's ills. I prayed, called the hospital, and spoke with her. It was vital that she knew that I loved her.

Many transitions transpired in my life that year, one of which my son and godson faced death daily while serving in Iraq. Mother, Elizabeth, Tomika and her unborn child also faced death. I was not in the best of health; therefore, my stressed level had increased tremendously. My journey was becoming traumatic, but *God delivers on time.*

4

God Warns His Children

God warns His children. Early one morning, God showed me a dream of Aunt Louise dressed in white linen. I shared the dream with Reather, but she did not comment. She knows that God communicates to me in dreams and visions and often said, "Do not dream about me."

"And to her was granted that she should be arrayed in fine linen, clean and white: for the fine linen is the righteousness of saints." Revelation 19: 8

God appointed angel carried Mrs. Louise Flowers' spirit to the presence of God in Paradise on March 31, 2005. Her spirit also settled in our hearts, where Jesus resides. Mother and I attended her home going celebration in Pittsburgh, Pennsylvania. Mother grieved for her sister, and I was concerned. At the cemetery, I had a day vision of Mother sleeping in a casket. Consequently, I knew that God's appointed angel would soon carry her spirit to the presence of God where her sister resided. I was overwhelmed and cried profusely. We loved auntie, but God loved her best. After eating at the church, we returned to Reather's home. Then, we returned to Lima. *God delivers on time.*

One night, God showed me a vision of Mother standing in my bedroom doorway dressed in white linen smiling at me, and then she vanished. Afterward, I recalled having a similar dream of auntie, and I knew what that vision implied. God was preparing me; however, I went into denial. I could not imagine mom not being in my life. When previous illnesses beset her, God spoke to her about continuing the work of the ministry. He would then manifest healing and deliverance in her body with an increased anointing to bless others. I remembered that trend. Then, I tried to bargain with God by reminding Him of how He had used her for the work of the ministry. Suddenly, I remembered the dream and vision, and I felt discontent. Then, I asked God not to take her from me. In addition, if her time on earth was ending, do not allow her to die at home. I did not want to see her laying in a pool of blood. Tomika has the gift of discernment, and she sees in the supernatural. Each time I had a vision of Mother passing, I called her. In the meantime, I waited for God to speak to Mother.

On a Saturday morning, I was listening to a minister preach on television. Mother walked out of my bedroom and said, "good morning." Suddenly, she started to speak in her Heavenly language.

"Jackie, God spoke to me and said that He answered your prayer," she prophesied.

I wondered which part of my prayer God had answered. I really knew; however, my denial state enabled me from accepting God's answer to my prayer. In the meantime, I enrolled in Penn Foster Career School, studying Medical Coding and Billing. I needed to occupied my mind with positive thoughts and obtain a career certificate.

One morning, I was in extreme pain and could not drive Mother for medical testing. Keesha agreed to drive her; however, they were taking long to return home. I called to discover that they were having fun. They had shopped and eaten. They would be home soon, and I was not to worry. God had blessed their quality time together.

Tomika's doctor admitted her into the hospital for an emergency cesarean, and we prayed. Beautiful Mikalah Renee entered this world on June 4. Their children including Kevin, Camrin, and Marquis were happy to learn that mom and sister were fine. Mother and I were excited because God had answered our prayers. Later, we visited with them and praised God for His blessing. *God delivers on time.*

God blessed me to celebrate unknowingly my last birthday with Mother at Arthur and Arnitia (Neet) Edward's home on July 4. We had great food and lots of fun. Unfortunately, Mother got sick. Neet's nursing skills returned, and she provided care. Once Mother felt better, I teased her about not being able to hang with me, the kid. We all laughed, knowing that she would respond.

"Shut up, Jackie. Neet, you better get her and make her leave me alone."

From Iraq, Todochi ordered a birthday card, flowers, and balloons for my birthday, and I was excited. I left them in our family room and later went to bed. While I was sleeping, somehow my balloons entered my bedroom, awakened me, and rubbed my face. I could not understand how that happened. Was something happening in the supernatural?

I later contacted Mother's doctor and drove her there for a check up. He recommended that her cancer specialist examine her for precaution. He wanted her seen by an Optometrist. Then, she had eye surgery. He wanted her seen by a nose, ear and throat specialists because her body fluids had started to drip. Her journey to the presence of God had begun. In other words, earth was calling her body from where it had come from, dust. He prescribed medications. Sometimes our doctor ordered tests that required fasting, so I fasted along with her. Sometimes, we ate out afterward and later returned home. *God delivers on time.*

God had blessed us with a case of greens. I disliked worms, so Mother cleaned them for me. Her cleaning solution consists of filling the sink with warm water and plenty of salt. Then, place small amounts of green in there. If worms or bugs were there, the salt would kill them. Remember that salt kills and purifies. One day, I followed her instruction; however, I noticed a fat green worm crawling on top of the greens, and I almost fainted. During that period, Mother was living across town, so I called Sister Clara to come rescue me. When she finally arrived, she offered to kill the worm and clean my greens; however, I had a better idea. After she killed the worm, drive my greens to mom, so she could clean them for me. I thought Sister Clara would die from laughter; however, I was serious. She killed the worm and bagged the greens. I drove us to Mother's place. After we arrived there, Mother and Sister Clara laughed at me. Mother also shook her head. Then, Sister Clara and I returned home.

Keesha later gave us cases of greens. This time, my faith was about to be tested. Mother mentioned this would be her last time cleaning greens for me, so she re-educated me.

"Fill your sink with plenty of salt and warm water. Then, place small amounts of green in there. The salt will kill worms, bugs, anything that is in there. Remember that salt purifies," she said.

Mother left for her bedroom. She was trying to prepare me for her home going; however, my denial state enabled me to focus. While she was gone, I placed a hammer nearby, incase I saw a worm. I know this sounds drastic, but what can I say. I managed to wash, bag and placed them in our freezer. I think the reason that worm survived before because too many greens were in my sink; therefore, he crawled to the top to remain alive. *God delivers on time.*

Mother revisited the kitchen with exhilaration and increased energy. Her face was glowing; her eyes sparkled. God had renewed her spirit. She had become as a little child. God's appointed angel would soon carry her spirit into the presence of God in Paradise.

"Verily I say unto you, Who soever shall not receive the kingdom of God as a little child, he shall not enter therein." *Mark 10:15*

Mother never dismissed the thought of living alone again and mentioned this to her other children. She had been an independent woman most of her life, never allowing anyone to provide or care for her. She wanted to have that experience one more time and gave it her best shot.

"Jackie, I feel good. I have not felt this good in a long time. By the way, who said I had to live with you anyway?"

"Your doctor, mom, but if you think that you can live alone again, I will contact her and your case manager to see what they say. I will not depend on others to care for you."

God had another plan. Our family doctor had returned from maternity leave. She did not know how ill Mother had become until she reviewed her unfavorable medical report results. Then, she went into shock. Her eyes were teary. She finally informed us that Mother had an abdominal aneurysm that could rupture at any moment. I was shocked. She then suggested a nursing home facility. When I could speak, I declined her suggestion. Immediately, she ran out of the examination room, leaving us along. I located her and asked how much time did Mother have to live? She could not reply. I then noticed how close they had become because she was crying. She finally managed to give me her direct telephone number, so our family could contact her if we had questions. Mother walked behind me, asked to use the restroom, and a nurse assisted her. God strengthen me again to keep my natural mind and to drive us home. I was then the barrier of sad news. I contacted my siblings and gave them the unfavorable news. Mother's time spent on earth was ending soon. *God delivers on time.*

The warning was about to be confirmed. One Sunday morning, I felt Mother's presence in my bedroom doorway, just as I had envisioned. A strange feeling came over me. Somehow, I knew that God had spoken to her.

"Jackie, are you sleeping?"

"No mom."

"I have heard from God. When the Lord calls me, I am going to answer, 'Yes,' to His call. I am going home to be with the Lord. Do you hear me talking to you?"

"I heard you, mom," I finally replied.

"Ok, but you did not answer me," was her reply.

Mother walked away. The final warning had transpired about her home going. My bargaining was no avail. God was not changing His mind; therefore, I came out of denial. My heart felt as if it would stop beating. I buried my face in my pillow and cried. I wanted to scream, 'please God do not take Mother from me.' In the meantime, God strengthened me to carry out His plan and purpose for her life.

Later one night, Mother awakened me, and she asked me to come to her bedroom. She gave me a small yellow flashlight, a red portable radio, and many batteries. She never wanted me to be without these items in case of a storm or an emergency. She knew that her appointed time was approaching. She was tire of doctors, hospitals and clinic visits; therefore, she insisted that I cancel all of her doctor appointments.

"Doctors are our helpers because they cannot heal us. Only Jesus can heal us. But, one day, I will have my new body," she said.

Immediately, I grabbed the telephone and rescheduled her appointments for the following year. Then, she thanked me for being her caregiver. She said that I had done a great job. She knew the sacrifices that I had made, and that God was going to bless me. We apologized for many misunderstandings. At that moment, God's grace, mercy and unconditional love made everything right between us. We talked and laughed; however, God would not allow further bonding. He knew it would be harder for me to let go. I later learned that during Mother's five-year mission in Lenoir, North Carolina, God had blessed her to meet Evangelist Ronnie and Jean Moore, special saints of God. She shared with Sister Moore that God had appointed me as her caregiver until He called her home; however, Mother never disclosed that information to me.

Mother frequently spoke in her Heavenly language. Her spirit was calmer. God's anointing had taken her above all illnesses with hardly any pain. It did not matter any way because no sickness was stopping her from obeying God's call to the work of the ministry. She loved serving God, which consisted of preaching, laying on of hands, prophesying, and praying for others as well as for me. In the meantime, exhaustion was taking its toll on her weak delicate body. Her strength was slowly leaving her. The Holy Spirit later guided me in keeping her at home from church services, and she agreed. Her willingness to obey God continued. She often said, "When God tells you to do anything, just do it." Afterward, God increased her telephone ministry. She prayed for people at all hours of the night and all over the United States of America. Sometimes I did not want them calling our home so she could rest; however, God would not permit me to interfere in His work. Her mission was not complete yet.

My nephew Raymond Wilson called, and God used him to speak to us. She obeyed God and imparted the mantle to me to carry on the Lord's work in her place. For me to accept and carry her mantle was honorable, but frightening. I did not want to walk her path on this earth; however, God had ordained that decision, not Jackie. He would not manifest this mantle within me until I went through trials and tribulations, and passed the test. Remember, we have to pass the test for our promotion to the next spiritual stage. The manifestation of God's anointing to bless others is not free, but thank God, salvation is because of Jesus death, burial, and resurrection. *God delivers on time.*

God had warned Reather about coming to visit Mother. She rushed here thinking it was mom's birthday weekend. She was shocked to learn that it was Samuel's birthday August 13. Mother was not surprised at seeing her there because she had a message for her.

"When God calls me, I am going home to be with the Lord. I am waiting on Him," she said.

In spite of the situation, we took pictures, ate, and talked about the old days. Reather later returned home with a saddened heart.

Mother was turning 82 on August 19, 2005. Jenera invited us to celebrate Mother's birthday early at Cracker Barrel Old Country Store, Inc. The food was fantastic. She loved their pinto beans, catfish, and cornbread. She received many gifts, cards including funds. We took pictures and had a joyous time. Then, she mentioned going shopping at Wal-Mart Shopping Center. When anyone mentioned going shopping at Wal-Mart, Mother's face would light up. Almost all of the cashiers knew her as

Mother Wilson at that store. One day, I drove Jenera and Mother there, and they shopped all day. She allowed mom to buy whatever she wanted, and they had a glorious time. Jenera always provided great care for Mother; however, she could no longer remain her aide. I believe she had gotten too close and or she went into denial about Mother passing soon. *God delivers on time.*

Keesha, her family, a guest, and I celebrated Mother's birthday at the Golden Corral Restaurant. The waiters sang, "Happy Birthday" to mom. The food was fantastic.

She received many gifts, cards including funds. We took pictures and had a great time. Mother had two birthday celebrations that year; however, we did not know that this would be her last.

Tomika attended Pioneer Career and Technology Center. She is a State Tested Nursing Assistant (STNA). She was also attending North Central State College, concentrating in nursing. She always gave me great advice. One day, I mentioned that parts of Mother's body had turned white; however, she thought I had lost my mind. She had never heard of a dying person walking and mottling at the same time. One night she had a supernatural experience, and she told me to spend lots of time with granny. She spoke with Mother frequently, and mom always prayed for her. One weekend, Marcus, Tomika and their family visited us. Mother spiritually bonded with Mikalah. She kissed and loved on her last great-granddaughter. Mikalah smiled, which made Mother's day.

"Mikalah, great-granny forgot to give you her telephone number, so you can call anytime you want to," great-granny stated.

Marcus was listening to Mother's conversation with his daughter; however, he had the strangest look on his face. It was as if he wondered why Mother had made that statement to her. I then suggested that Tomika cook dinner like the one we used to enjoy years ago. Initially, she wanted to go home, but Marcus was not ready. I believe that was a part of God's plan. A burst of energy suddenly hit Tomika, and she started to cook. She did not want either granny or I in the kitchen because we were in her way. Her food was great as always. Mother did not need her teeth to eat. I did not realize that Tomika was cooking her last family meal. God blessed their special time together. Later, Keesha's daughter Chardenay and other family members arrived to eat. Chardenay loved great-granny and vice versa. She reminded her of Keesha when she was a baby. God blessed their special time together. Todochi called from Iraq and spoke with his granny. He loved her and vice versa. God blessed their special time over the telephone. She assured him that he would be coming home.

"Everything is gonna be alright," her favorite quote was.

Mother retained her life insurance policy premiums. She believed that everyone should have life or burial insurance and not leave a burden on your family. We should prepare to live and prepare to die. She had preplanned her home going arrangements four years ago. She wanted the viewing and celebration on the same day to make this event easier for our family. She chose a beautiful designer rose casket and a suit to match it. I placed her burial apparel in a garment bag and hung it at the back of my closet. She tried to convince me to style her hair; however, that was not happening. I could not imagine shampooing, blow drying and curling her hair, and definitely not that of a corpse head. She laughed; however, I did not think her request was comical. She finally agreed to allow her cosmetology Ms. Emma McNeal to style her hair, and I was happy. They shared a spiritual bond. She loved Emma and Bonnie and vice versa. She allowed mom to minister to clients at her salon. She once styled her hair in our home because I was unable to drive her to the salon. During one of my hospital admission, she drove mom to visit me. After my discharge, she drove her to my home. Emma was like a daughter to Mother. She was our family. *God delivers on time.*

Mother loved the McFadden, Bradley, and Jones families, and they loved her. They shared a spiritual bond. Before we moved in together, Minister Alfred Lewis Jones I drove mom to church. God used her to impart His Word in their spirits and to prophesy. After God had confirmed her home going, she organized her celebration program. She requested a special song by Sister LaDonna Jones, "Walk Around Heaven." She wanted Minister Alfred

Lewis Jones II to render the music. She enjoyed his playing and singing. I spoke with Sister LaDonna Jones, and she agreed to participate. The Jones family and Mother had no problem praising God. They were not quenching the Spirit. Mother wanted us to give God the praise, glory, and honor by thanking Him for what He had done. She wanted us to dance (shout) and have an attitude of gratitude.

"In everything give thanks; for this is God's will for you in Christ Jesus." First Thessalonians 5:18   God delivers on time.

Mother loved Curtis Knuckles because he was a son to her. They shared a spiritual bond. God often sent her to different states for the work of the ministry, and he moved her there. She could always depend on him. She imparted God's Word into his spirit.

Mother made a great impact in the life of many. People never forgot "Mother Wilson." They had positive things to say about God's dwelling Spirit within her. She loved God, and she would never compromise His Word. She would tell you when you were wrong.

God warns His children; however, it is up to us to listen, acknowledge, and obey what the Spirit is saying to us. *God delivers on time.*

5

The Detachment Process

The detachment process begins. Before your rebirth spirit returns to Paradise, God will detach you from your family and loved ones. During the separation process, you may not understand what is happening. You may even go into denial, but God does the separating. *God delivers on time.*

God appointed angel carried Mr. Clyde Roger Sr., spirit to the presence of God in Paradise on September 6, 2005. His spirit also settled in our hearts, where Jesus resides. Mother was too ill to travel for his home going celebration. I wrote a letter on her behalf and enclosed a poem from me. We loved Clyde, but God loved him best.

God appointed angel carried my great-aunt Mrs. Martha Littlejohn Border's spirit to the presence of God in Paradise on September 18, 2005. Her spirit also settled in our hearts, where Jesus resides. She was 94 years old. She was the last of the Littlejohn generation. She and I had similar birth dates, July 4; therefore, we shared a special bond. I called to wish her, "Happy Birthday" yearly until God detached us. Once again, we could not attend another home going celebration because of Mother's illnesses. As before, I wrote a letter and enclosed a poem. We loved Aunt Martha, but God loved her best.

Samuel called and spoke with our mother on October 9.

"Mama's voice sounds strong," he often said.

Inez was planning a surprise home visit; however, that visit was not in God's plan. Mother told her that she would be here for me because she was stronger now.

Isaiah called us on October 10. Mother prophesied to him. Raymond called our mother daily. He loved her. He was concerned about her health issues.

"What are you doing, little bit young lady," he asked.

Raymond referring to our mother as a young person, always made her day. Mother had given all of her children to God. She knew that He would take care of us. In the meantime, God had detached her from us.

The Holy Spirit directed me to invited Sister Clara to eat dinner with us on October 11. She and Mother were excited to see each other. Mother declared how much she loved her and vice versa. We had a beautiful fellowship. They hugged, ate and talked about God's divine will for one's life. In the meantime, she was exhibiting tiredness, so I insisted that she should go to bed and rest. I did not realize that I was about to be preached to. She said that I was trying to be her mother again, and she knew when to go to bed. She continued to fellowship; however, she had the strangest look on her face as if she wanted to tell us something. I think she wanted to say, "Good-bye" to Sister Clara, but she never did. Before she left, Mother held her tightly and reaffirmed how much she loved her. God detached them.

Todochi called from Iraq again and spoke with Mother on October 12. I remember her talking loudly to make sure that he could hear her. I assured her that he could and then she was satisfied. She reaffirmed that everything was going to be all right. He was coming home, and that she loved him. God detached them. Later, while we were gone, he called again. Sounding distressed, he left a message, stating that he was calling Keesha. I later heard an improvised device (Roadside bomb) had exploded. At this time, I did not know a Bravo was dead. I called and e-mailed military officials without success. I had forgotten that any time an attack occurred, there were no avenues of communication for 24 hours. I had to wait until someone contacted me. I was nervous; however, I never gave up on God's promise to keep my son safe. Earlier that day, I cooked black-eyed peas and made slaw. Later, Mother cooked the best cornbread and seven fish sticks. She prayed over our food, making sure we both had equal amounts of fish, and then we ate. We had unknowingly eaten our last supper together. Mother and I were fatigued, so we retired for the night.

The following morning was unusual. It was so quiet,

almost as if time had stopped. I had the weirdest feeling without an understanding of why. I heard no sound in Mother's bedroom. She was not walking through the house as usual, talking to baby (the turtle) or watching television. I called her private telephone, but she did not answer. I figured she had either passed or overslept. I had no idea of what to expect after I opened her bedroom door. I almost panic; however, the Holy Spirit reminded me that she would not die at home. Then, I asked God to prepare me for whatever lies ahead. Fearing the worst, (my human side) I opened her door to discover that she was looking for something.

"Mom, you frightened me to death. Lord woman, I thought you were dead in here. Why did you not answer your telephone? Do you know what time it is? You are going to be late for school. Thank God you were not dead in here!" I fearfully shouted.

"No, Jackie, I have not left yet. I forgot where I had put my phone. Oh, well, here it is; it was underneath my pillow. Lord have mercy, I have overslept. I am going to miss the bus. I have to shower. Will you pack my bag and put 4-8 ounce cups of water in the bottle for me?" she asked with much laughter.

"Yes, I will. I will drive you to school, so do not worry. But you better get a move on, girl."

Mother laughed as tears ran down her face on the way to our bathroom. I was also laughing, shaking and thanking God for her being found alive. She showered, dressed, and waited for the bus to pick her up, which was unusual. She always kept the bus driver waiting for her; however, she shocked him that morning. He commended her for being ready to leave on time. She was anxious to leave me, but I did not understand.

"Jackie, I'm gone, I love you. I'm gone!" She strongly repeated.

"Jackie, did you hear me?" She asked.

"Ok, mom, I can hear."

"But you did not answer me."

"Ok, mom, see you later, love you, too."

At that time, I was confused. I could not understand why she used the expression, "gone." She often said, "I am leaving now, see you this evening. I love you."

Unknowingly, our last earthly laugh and conversation had concluded. In the meantime, I was extremely restless. I thought my anxiety was from waiting for a military representative or Todochi to contact me about the bombing that had taken place in Iraq.

The detachment process in the physical realm was on its way to being complete. *God delivers on time.*

6

Mother's Home Going

Mother's home going was about to transpire. She tried to prepare me for her home going after the passing of her mom, Mrs. Amanda Littlejohn Branan-Borders, 34 years ago without success. She mentioned that when your mother dies, a part of you also dies. When they lower her body in the grave, a part of you also goes in her grave. There is emptiness inside of you that only God can fill. The reason is that she carried you in her womb and later birthed you; therefore, you are a part of each other. Sometimes she cried for her mom, but the Holy Spirit comforted her. I tried mentally to prepare myself for her home going as well as others did; however, I could not relate because I had not walked behind her casket yet. God had the perfect plan. The Holy Spirit final preparations for me were in God's timing. Regardless of my trial or tribulation, God's love would sustain and see me through. He would use what Satan intended for evil to destroy me for my good to be a blessing to others.

Later, Lorain Lovett called from the Elderly Daycare Center to inform me that Mother had fainted. The ambulance was there, and I needed to come now. I knew then why I had been feeling so strangely. At that moment, God begin preparing me for her home going. The Holy Spirit directed my steps. He instructed me to drive to St. Rita's Medical Center instead of the Center, and I mentioned this to Lorain. I dressed, called Inez, and she started to cry. I mentioned that Mother would be alright. She had to be strong for me because I was driving to the hospital alone. I told her to notify our siblings, and I would call her after I arrived at the hospital. The Holy Spirit had strengthened me to console her. I called Tomika, but without success. At that time, I could not remember Keesha's work telephone number. I finally contacted Sister Dorothy, and she declared that she would meet me at the hospital soon. I connected with Roxie, and she prayed for my strength. No one was telling me what I wanted to hear, which was, "Mother Wilson is going to be alright."

Instead, the Holy Spirit prepared me to meet the people by taking my spirit to the supernatural; yet I was here no earth. He ministered to my soul and spirit. I had to rely on God's Word, let go and allow Him to do what He considered necessary to move me forward without Mother. He reminded me that I would see Mother again, and we would forever be with the Lord.

MOTHER'S HOME GOING

"16 For the Lord himself shall descend from heaven with a shout, with the voice of the archangel, and with the trump of God: and the dead in Christ shall rise first: 17 Then we which are alive and remain shall be caught up together with them in the clouds, to meet the Lord in the air: and so shall we ever be with the Lord.18 Wherefore comfort one another with these words."
1 Thessalonians 4:16-18

After I arrived at the hospital, I noticed Lorain sitting near the doorway of Mother's room. She reached out to me, and we embraced. I cried on her shoulder, but the Holy Spirit comforted me. Todd A. Bell, D.O., an emergency room physician and I met. I gave him mom's medical profile, which included doctor names, a list of medications, her allergies and other pertinent information. I believe that everyone should have a synopsis of their medical information for emergencies or doctor visits. I typed ours years ago and kept them in my purse. Sometimes, you have to update them; nevertheless, I like the convenience.

Dr. Bell introduced me to Chaplin Tom Niese, who was/is a Catholic Priest. Chaplin Niese, Lorain, and I walked to the family room. My siblings located St. Rita's telephone number; however, I had to be the barrier of bad news. Our mother was dying.

"Tell Mother, I am on my way, wait for me. I am coming, please wait on me," Inez cried.

Samuel knew our mother was passing because he felt extreme pain in his head. The Holy Spirit reminded me of where Keesha worked, and a nurse contacted her. Later,

Diana Bishop, Executive Director for Counsel On Aging arrived. Dr. Bell then informed us that Mother was waiting for me because it was time to say good-bye. Chaplin Niese, Lorain, and Diana accompanied me to Mother's bedside. Her guardian angel was there to carry her spirit to her destination of certainty, Paradise (Heaven). She stared upward at the corner of the emergency room and never blinked her eyes. I placed my face on hers and began to cry, opening my mouth without knowing what to say. Suddenly, my spirit cried to hers.

"Mom, I love you so much. I love you so much. I love you so very much. You said when the Lord called you home, you would answer, 'Yes' to His call.' I am going to be alright mom. Go into God's presence now. We will see each other again."

Chaplin Niese prayed by thanking God for Mother's time spent here working for Him et cetera. He commended her spirit back to God. My eyes opened, and I noticed tears running from her motionless eyes, down the side of her face.

Before the foundation of this world, the Most High God chose Sarah Mae Branan as His royal priesthood daughter. He knew her while she was in Mrs. Amanda Littlejohn Branan's womb. He wonderfully and beautifully made her in His image and likeness. God had chosen and ordained her for His plan and a purpose. He had given her a destiny. She accepted His drawing for salvation and sanctification, and for the work of the ministry. She also accepted His call to be with Him.

MOTHER'S HOME GOING

God appointed angel carried our mother Ms. Sarah Mae Wilson's spirit to the presence of God in Paradise on October 13, 2005. Her spirit also settled in our hearts, where Jesus resides.

HEAVEN IS A MUST

God granted Sarah M. Wilson eternal rest,
Because He knew what was best.
His grace, love, and mercy made everything right,
So she could enter Paradise.

She did not resist God's perfect plan,
Given that, she had viewed the Promised Land.
She peacefully accepted His Will for her life,
Because He was her guiding light.

She is arrayed in fine linen, clean, and white,
Because God's proclamation was right.
Today her spirit and soul is at rest,
We love her, but God loved her best.

Mother's spirit is in God's presence.
Her body is returning to dust.
But… if we want to see her again,
Heaven is a must.

My God Delivers On Time

God is Sovereign. He is the Supreme Creator and Ruler. He is our Heavenly Father and Mother, Best Friend, and our All in All. God chooses His Servant Kings and Priests to fulfill His plan and purpose. After God changes me from mortality to immortality, I will tease Mother about God's choice of using a Catholic Priest's prayer of commendation and entrustment to carry out His plan for her eternal life.

Our mother's home going happened. She left us from this realm; however, we will see her again. Most importantly, the Holy Spirit will never leave or forsake us. *God delivers on time.*

7

The Devastation

The home going of our mother was devastating. Charles and Keesha arrived at the hospital to discover that Mother had passed. They were devastated and grieved. Sister Dorothy came and Charles told her that Mother had passed. She knew the closeness we shared; therefore, she was concerned. Upon entering Mother's room, she realized that God was strengthening me to go through the most difficult time of my life. I was not myself, but the Holy Spirit was comforting me. I was consoling others, including Arnitia Edwards. I later laid my face on Mother's motionless body, loving her in death. I combed her hair and kissed her repeatedly, asking her silently.

"Why did you leave me, girl? You have been my father and mother, sister-in-Christ and best friend as long as I can remember. What am I going to do without you loving me?" My heart ached; however, I remembered someone trying to comfort me.

'Mother Wilson is in Heaven now. She won't have to suffer no more. She would not want you to cry, but be strong. You also have to be strong for others.' In the meantime, I had to take care of Mother's remaining business. I spoke with her cardiologist and other doctors, and they offered their condolences. Later, from Jones/Clark Funeral Home, a representative arrived to get her remains. I saw a black body bag on their mortuary cot carrying her body down the hallway. Instantly, I had a flashback of grandma in that same manner. The reality of her passing was inescapable. My emotions got the best of me, and I screamed. Many nurses rescued me with prayer and love. They were my angel nurses. Later, we walked outside to wait for our cars, so we could leave for home. Suddenly, I saw the hearse carrying her remains toward the funeral home, so her body could be prepared for her home going celebration. The next time we saw her would be at a private viewing for our approval. I cried again; however, Mr. Johnny Hall comforted me.

"Your mother is still with us. Everything is gonna be alright," he said.

After I arrived home, Keesha drove my devastated grieving grandchildren to our home, where I consoled them. Ann Ackles, an employee of the Elderly Daycare Center mentioned that Mother preached her last message before passing.

'God is speaking to His people, but they are not listening. You must be born again to enter the Kingdom of God,' was what she said.

Mother had accomplished God's plan, purpose, and destiny for her life, which was God's Perfect Will. Our family thanks Chaplin Niese, Dr. Bell, St. Rita's staff, Lorain Lovett, Diana Bishop, my angel nurses for your prayers and empathy shown at the passing of our mother. *God delivers on time.*

Keesha was the person in charge. She contacted our remaining family and others too numerous to mention. Inez was devastated; nevertheless, with the help of her son, Curtis, she managed to fly to Lima with much grief in her heart. She had previously buried her husband and now our mother. She called Tomika, who was extremely devastated, grieved, and fainted. She and her family came later to Lima. She contacted the Red Cross and Sergeant Derek Hunker, so they could notify Todochi. The military prepared him to fly home. Mother passing spread quickly. My telephone was a hotline. Pastor Dr. H. Frank Taylor III called, and he was shocked at the news of Mother passing; nevertheless, he agreed to present her eulogy. Mrs. Helen (Mama Helen) Roberts came with a large bag of collard green; however, Inez cleaned them for us. Many individuals came to our home with food and sadness. They understood the closeness Mother and I had shared. They tried to comfort me, although, I had to put some of them out of our home. We are private individuals. We seldom socialized with people; therefore, I was not use to having that many folks in our home. Later, that night, I had a migraine headache. Tomika checked my blood pressure and insisted that I go immediately to the hospital. I finally agreed. We discovered that I had a mini stroke (TIA-Transient Ischemic Attack). The doctor later discharged me. *God will deliver me on time.*

The following day, Coleman Clark came to finalize Mother's arrangement, and he was very helpful. He also visited with us daily. I called Emma; however, she was grief stricken and could not style Mother's hair. She was family. Daily, she visited with me, and I appreciate her for taking the time to come to our home. Previously, Sister Dorothy Knuckles was Mother's beautician. I contacted her, and she agreed to style her hair.

I had forgotten to include Mother's shoes in her garment bag, so Inez chose a pair for her. Later, our family had a previewing at the funeral home. After the initial shock of seeing her in the casket was over, God strengthen us. Mother looked beautiful. Clark did a great job in applying her makeup. Sister Dorothy did a great job in styling her hair and gluing on her beautiful designer fingernails matching her suit. We took many pictures. Since Mother had requested no public viewing at the funeral home, we were thankful to have had that time of privacy with her. I was happy that she had already taken care of business because it made this process easier. Preplanning your (possible home going) is the smartest decision a person can make. The reason I parenthesized possible home going is because not all individuals will sleep (die), but we shall all be changed.

"Behold, I shew you a mystery; We shall not all sleep, but we shall all be change." First Corinthians 15:51

Mother had an awesome home going celebration on October 18. Minister Jones II sang most of her favorite songs; for instance, "Cant Nobody Do Me Like Jesus" and "God Is Not Dead. The Holy Spirit anointed Sister LaDonna Jones to sing Mother's requested song, "Walk Around Heaven." She was a blessing to others. Brother Brian Jones along with Sister Clara White danced for the Lord. They knew Mother served God and was a blessing to others. At that moment, I almost forgot about her passing. Suddenly, Coleman Clark walked toward her casket to close it. He asked Inez and me to come forward, and we wondered why? Coleman wanted me to cover Mother's body with her blanket. In the meantime, he was having difficulty unlocking her diamond and pearl watch. He finally succeeded and hand it to me. Inez then suggested that my earrings remain on our mother. Huh, I wondered why she suggested mines and not hers. Well, anyway, I agreed. I then covered her body with her blanket, and Coleman assisted Inez with lowering her in the casket. The difficult part occurred when he closed her casket. Every imaginable emotion silently overwhelmed me. Mother's body, an empty shell was no longer available for me to see on this earth. My heart ached, and I had a terrible headache. I wanted to scream, but I had to be strong for others. Pastor Taylor did a great job in presenting her eulogy.

Following Mother's home going celebration, Coleman drove her body to Woodlawn Cemetery, her temporary physical destination. I watched her casket slowly being let down into her beautiful matching designer rose vault that had her identification information on the top of it. The most difficult part was watching the workers close her grave. Afterward, I was devastated. I understood what Mother tried to convey to me concerning her mom's home going and burial. When she passed, a part of me died. When they buried her, a part of me went in her grave. We were and will always be a part of each other. I felt alone in my spirit. I felt that void, emptiness. Brother Knuckles asked if I wanted to watch the worker close her grave; however, I could not leave until they placed her beautiful flowers on her gravesite. Then, I had completed what God had ordained me to do, which was to care for our mother until He call her home and see that she had a proper burial. Mother's body returned to earth (dust) from where it came from, her spirit unto God who gave it.

"Then shall the dust return to the earth as it was: and the spirit shall return unto God who gave it." Ecclesiastes 12:7

Coleman's representative escorted us back to the Limousine. Then, we returned to the church for a repast. Our family provided the food and sisters-in-Christ cooked for us. Their hospitality and food were fantastic. Our family thanks you. After we returned home, Inez discovered that Clark's workers had brought some of Mother's flowers to our home. We did not know what they were thinking; nevertheless, they returned them. The following morning, we met at the hotel restaurant where my siblings stayed. We had prayer and ate breakfast. We tried to fellowship, but our hearts were sad. Later, my siblings with the exception of Inez returned home. My god sister Clara also stayed with me. *God delivers on time.*

Mother's first year in Paradise was overwhelming for me. My grieving process was not going well. Satan recognized my grief stricken state, and he set me up to devour. I no longer kept her home going on the spiritual level, but allowed it to remain and rest in the physical realm. It was hard for me to go to church without Mother, but Keesha insisted. Inez and I attended Charles and Keesha's church and everyone was supportive.

My anger enabled me from praying and meditating on God's Word, so I could move forward without mother. I could not receive the saints encouragement. I was angry with God for taking Mother away from me. As a result, unforgiveness had sneaked in my heart against God for her passing.

First, Mother residing in Heaven did not comfort me. Secondly, she did not suffer because the anointing had taken her spirit to the supernatural realm without pain, so she could complete the work of her ministry. In the meantime, I felt that I had to put a mask on, so people would think that I was fine. My mind was in a battle and only God could heal and deliver me. I grieved for Mother, daily. I started to visit her gravesite frequently. My stressed level increased. I started having mini strokes and migraine headaches again. My doctor diagnosed me with a bone marrow expansion and a blockage in my brain. I was in and out of the hospital. Brother and Sister Knuckles, Arnitia, Derek, his mom, Anna and many other were there with me. Saints were praying nationwide. Later, I begin to feel better. Then, Inez and Sister Clara returned to their destinations. Todochi mentioned that he could stay home with me. I discerned that he wanted to rejoin his fellow troops in Iraq; therefore, I released him. Immediately, he left for the airport. Now, I was at home alone, devastated while trying to face reality of her home going, but without God's active Word in my life. Our house was no longer a home, but a place of sorrow. Everything in it reminded me that Mother was no longer there; nevertheless, I managed to give some of her items to people she instructed me to. I disliked looking in her bedroom, so I closed the door. I had become selfish. Then, I stopped going to church because I was tired of pretending to be strong and that everything was fine.

The holiday seasons were approaching without a clue of how to handle Mother's absence. For me to shop at her favorite store Wal-Mart Shopping Center and eat at her favorite restaurants, Golden Corral and Cracker Barrel Old

Country Store, Inc were overwhelming, so I stayed away. In the meantime, Thanksgiving without her was devastating. The weather was snowy, cold and icy. I did not cook, but remained in bed. Keesha insisted that I come to her house to eat, but I declined. I was depressed and exhausted. In the meantime, Sakeyna convinced me to come, but her driving in the snow was fearful. After we arrived at Keesha's house, she noticed my weight lost; however, I was unaware that I had stopped eating. I was also unaware that a spirit of grief had consumed me. Later, Todochi called from Iraq and made my day. Then, my sister Elizabeth Monford's spirit entered the presence of God in Paradise on December 17, 2005. Her spirit also settled in our hearts, where Jesus resides. I attend her home going celebration with much sadness in my heart. Beverly allowed me to speak words of encouragement to my extended family. (Thank you Beverly)

Christmas without Mother was depressing and devastating. I missed her smiles when opening presents, taking pictures, joking, and laughing. She never had to cook. We just pigged out (ate) talked with my siblings and others, and slept. She always enjoyed her grandchildren, great-grand children, and me.

New Years without Mother was very sad and devastating. She always prayed five minutes before the New Year came in. Then, we welcomed in the New Year together. I would have cooked black-eye peas and collard greens… I missed her so much. I was happy when the holiday seasons had passed. In the meantime, I vowed not to celebrate any holiday seasons at my home ever again.

Samuel's mother-in-law, Mrs. Icilda Weslenda Halstead spirit entered the presence of God in Paradise on January 14, 2006. Her spirit also settled in our hearts, where Jesus resides. She was a second mom to all of us. I wrote a poem because I was ill again and could not attend her home going ceremony.

St. Rita's Pastoral, Patient Relation Staff, and volunteers invited us to an Interfaith Memorial Service in remembrance of Mother and others that had crossed over on April 24. This was a reflective moment. We prayed, lit candles, and sang songs. There was an informal reception following the service. Our family thanks St. Rita's Hospital.

Isaiah's wife Mrs. Carolynn Wilson spirit entered the presence of God in Paradise on May 4, 2006. Her spirit also settled in our hearts, where Jesus resides. I was still ill and could not attend her home going celebration; however, I later visited with him and our remaining family in Pittsburgh, PA.

One evening, I forgot that Mother had passed. I grabbed the telephone to call her, remembered, and was devastated. I called Reather, and she had a similar experience about her Mother. We both cried; however, she gave me information. I needed healing from Mother's passing.

Even in the midst of my storms, God was/is good,

all the time. God blessed the Bravo Company 612th Engineer Battalions Unit to return stateside (USA). I praise God's Holy name.

My journey was devastating, but *God delivers on time.*

8

Bravo Company 612th Engineer Battalion Unit

The Task Force Iron Claw organized the Ohio Army National Guard Bravo Company 612th Engineer Battalion unit. Their bases are located in Fremont and Tiffin, Ohio. My son Todochi and my godson Derek were a part of that unit. *God delivers on time.*

Please allow me to refresh your memory: Following 9-11, from the oval office desk, President George W. Bush announced that weapons of mass destruction existed in Iraq that threatened our nation's security. After bombing Iraq, our troops revealed there were no weapons of mass destruction found in Iraq. Terrorism and sectarian warfare was threatening to tear Iraq apart. A war to disarm a state was no longer pertinent. Our troop's mission then became a fight against insurgency. They shifted tactics to protect the Iraqi people, trained their Security Forces, while taking out terrorist leaders. They fought block by block to help

Iraq seize the chance for a better future.

The Bravo Company's primary mission was to guarantee that the main supply routes throughout Baghdad's areas of operations remained free of improvised explosive devices (IED). Their accomplishments were great in magnitude. The Task Force Iron Claw cleared more than 17, 000 kilometers of roadway and found 92 improvised explosive devices on 331 combat patrols. As a whole, they found over 300 improvised explosive devices while patrolling over 62,000 km of Baghdad roadway on 990 combat patrols.

The military had assigned the Bravo other missions before their time of deployment was completed. They were responsible for the Task Force Iron Claw Academy. This academy became the 3rd Infantry Division training standard for new route clearance teams upon arrival to Iraq. The Bravo Company, with the assistance of other companies in the Battalion trained 12 classes totaling 432 students.

The Assault and Obstacle platoon (A & O) tasked with numerous force protection missions and totally emplaced over 23, 450 concrete barriers on Camp Liberty vehicle checkpoints surrounding Baghdad. Their efforts greatly improved the force protection and thus the survivability of United States and Iraqi troops alike.

At the infamous Abu Ghuraib prison, for two months, the military assigned the 1st Platoon to a Force Protection detail. They were responsible for tower guard security on the north side of the prison complex. A high value target for insurgent attacks throughout their deployment remained there.

The Bravo Company, other Platoons, and civilian's resilience enabled the Iraqi people to embrace a new destiny, even though many challenges remain. Our troops, the Iraqis and coalition forces together made great sacrifices. Nine Bravos including Sergeant Derek Hunker were recipients of the Purple Heart for receiving injuries because of enemy attacks. Sadly, to say Sergeant Jeremy M. Hodge was killed during an attack. **We Honor You!**

Ohio Army National Guard Bravo Company 612th Engineer Battalion unit had completed their mission in 2005. God blessed them to return stateside on January 8, 2006. The day of Todochi's homecoming, we visited Mother's gravesite. He laid down on her grave and cried. He was remembering her prophesy. 'You are coming home and everything is gonna be alright.' We cried, but the Holy Spirit comforted us. He loved granny because she played a major role in his life. He had missed approximately 14 months of not being in her life. He had mixed emotions; however, he was happy to be home. He had flashbacks and problem sleeping. I reminded him that God had blessed him to come home, and he was fine. Todochi, a Combat Engineer gave the Army National Guard a total of eight years, six active and two inactive. He will receive his Honorable Discharge Certificate.

Previously, Todochi had purchased a duplex that needed restoration, so he worked on his house. Even so, God blessed him to return to work. Marathon transferred him to Raleigh, North Carolina, Indianapolis, Indiana, and back to Findlay Ohio. We were happy to have him back in Ohio near us again. He is now attending Bowling Green University, furthering his education in Business Administration. God is good, all the time. *God delivers on time.*

God bless our troops for bringing hope of freedom to Iraq. We will share in the honors given them, as we were mentally with them in Iraq. War has wounded all veterans in some way; even so, we must never forget their dedication to Iraq as well as the United States of America. The (Bad Boyz) were "Tried and Proven." *God delivers on time.*

9

Satan's Attack

Let us be mindful of who Satan is. Satan is the father of all liars... Previously, Satan resided in Heaven, but tried to rule God's Kingdom. Then, he forfeited his stay and privilege to return there. He is crafty. He conned Eve and used her to manipulate Adam, and changed the course of God's original plan for us. Thank God, because of Jesus death, burial and resurrection, we can receive salvation and reside in Heaven forever. Now, Satan is angry with us. His first attempt is to *steal*, but his ultimate goal is to devour.

"The thief cometh not, but for to steal, and to kill, and to destroy." John 10:10

"Be sober, be vigilant; because your adversary the devil, as a roaring lion, walketh about, seeking whom he may devour" *1 Peter 5:8*

Unknowingly, I had allowed Satan an open door to my mind, and he dramatically attacked my thought pattern. Living without Mother was difficult for me because of the closeness we had shared. I missed her badly. My pain was great in magnitude. My heart ached.

Satan had my carnal mind locked. I was no longer clearheaded or watchful. Satan *stole* my desire to meditate on God's Word. He never intended God's active Word to remain in my life. As a result, I forgot God's promise that I would see Mother again. Satan *stole* my desire to assemble with the saints because they reminded me of Mother's home going. As a result, my support system no longer existed. Satan *stole* my joy. He never intended for me to be happy again. As a result, I went into a deep state of depression. Satan *stole* my peace of mind. I was angry with God for calling Mother home. As a result, he tormented my mind. Satan *stole* my will to live; however, God revealed this to Sister Moore, and she called and said, "You can not go home to be with your mother yet. You have to carry on the work of the ministry in her place." In the meantime, Satan still had a hold on my mind. He never intended for me to be a blessing to others or for God to bless me. As a result, he tried to hinder my God given destiny. Satan never intended for me to pursue the work of the ministry. He constantly reminded me of the price Mother had paid for her increased anointing to bless others. I did not want to pay that price. I had already gone through enough. As a result, a spirit of fear came upon me.

SATAN'S ATTACK

Satan had taken my mind into captivity, and he sought to devour my body. I continued to think about Mother's absence. Mother mentally remained on my mind. As as result, a spirit of grief controlled me. I grieved morning, noon, and night; no human could fill that emptiness. I went into a deeper state of depression. I had anxiety attacks, migraines and mini strokes frequently, resulting in many hospitalizations. I had numbness and weakness on my left side, causing me to undergo physical therapy to strengthen my motor skills. I had hair loss, slurred speech, blurred vision, nausea, sleepless nights, forgetfulness, and loss 40 pounds. On top of that, my glucose level was 69. My nurse administered glucose water. Normally, my blood pressure is 110/70, yet at one time, it exceeded 203/144. I used a daily high blood pressure patch and various medications, but without any success. I was born with infant veins. The nurses and technicians missed them frequently and that was very painful. I was tired of the IV's and shots. Seven specialists had seen me, and they provided care by using what they knew best, medication. I was exhausted and wanted to die. I told my children that if God did not manifest my healing, at least, I would see Mother and Jesus, and live with them forever; however, they never gave up.

My neurologist referred me to a specialist in Cleveland, Ohio. Keesha later drove us there; however, I had another mini stroke. We prayed. The doctor examined me and mentioned that I was over medicated and needed to exercise, daily. God did not create our bodies to accommodate or process a variety of chemicals. My family doctor and I needed to address my depression state by confronting the underline problems that were causing the migraine headaches. Then, my blood pressure would stabilize. After we returned to Lima, I thought about the problems that needed addressed. I started exercising daily. I walked up to three miles. At one point, I no longer needed high blood pressure medications; nevertheless, God was not through with me.

Remaining unfocused on God's Word will enable Satan to act out his first attempt, which is to steal. If our hearts are not guarded, the thief will steal God's active Word distracting us from remembering God's promises. He wants to weaken us and cancel our faith out. He will then gain control of our defeated minds without our knowledge. We will become stagnated, hopeless, in a state of dysfunction and wastefulness. He does not want us to experience God's divine anointing power or reach our destinies. He never wanted me to be joyous, healed, and delivered again. Let us be mindful that we wrestle not against flesh and blood…

"For we wrestle not against flesh and blood, but against principalities, against powers, against the rulers of the darkness of this world, against spiritual wickedness in high places." *Ephesians 6:12.*

We need knowledge of how Satan is winning some

storms. Satan wins storms because we lack knowledge of God's Word. Lack is a shortage, something absent.

"6 My people are destroyed for lack of knowledge: because thou hast rejected knowledge, I will also reject thee, that thou shalt be no priest to me: seeing thou hast forgotten the law of thy God, I will also forget thy children. 7 As they were increased, so they sinned against me: therefore will I change their glory into shame." Hosea 4:6   God delivers on time.

Satan wins storms because we have failed in the area of grace. Grace is a gift from God to humankind: Grace is God's infinite love, mercy, favor, and goodwill shown to humankind. Grace is freedom from past, present, and future sins through repentance to God. In Christianity, God's unmerited grace is sufficient for all who believe. He bestows His grace on whomever He pleases. Salvation is by grace. God has redeemed us through the blood of Jesus Christ. The very chief of sinners is not beyond the reach of His divine mercy. No one can claim it as his or her inalienable right. If grace is unearned and undeserved, then none is entitled to it. If grace is a gift, then none can demand it. Jesus accepts us for who we are and loves us unconditionally, not because we have done anything to deserve it, but because of His grace.

"But after that the kindness and love of God our Savior toward man appeared, not by works of righteousness which we have done, but according to his mercy he saved us, by the washing of regeneration, and renewing of the Holy Ghost; which he shed

on us abundantly through Jesus Christ our Savior; that being justified by his grace, we should be made heirs according to the hope of eternal life." Titus 3:4-7

Satan wins storms because we have failed in the area of faith. Faith is confidence, trust, belief, reliance, trustworthiness, and persuasion. It is to trust and believe in something or somebody, especially without logical proof. God has dealt every man a measure of faith.

"For I say, through the grace given unto me, to every man that is among you, not to think of himself more highly than he ought to think; but to think soberly according as God hath dealt to every man the measure of faith." Romans 12:3

In the New Testament faith is the divinely implanted principle of inward confidence, assurance, trust, and reliance in God and all that He says.

"1 Now faith is the substance of things hoped for, the evidence of things not seen. Hebrews 11:1-2

Satan wins storms because of a spirit of fear. God has not given us a spirit of fear.

"For God hath not given us the spirit of fear; but of power, and of love, and of a sound mind." 2 Timothy 1:7

Satan wins storms; nevertheless, he cannot win the battle. Battle is a large-scale fight between armed forces, armed fighting, or any fights or conflict. A battle could also be symbolic of an obstacle, hindrance, or insurmountionable problem. Our battles do not belong to us, but to God.

> *"And he said, Hearken ye, all Judah, and ye inhabitants of Jerusalem, and thou king Jehoshaphat, Thus saith the LORD unto you, Be not afraid nor dismayed (to make afraid at the prospect of trouble) by reason of this great multitude; for the battle is not yours, but God's."* 2 Chronicles 20:15

Satan and his attacks are real. He is a lying deceitful thief. My storm of grieving is coming to an end. God will give me the victory through our Lord Jesus Christ. Victory is a triumph, as conquest, succeed, and win.

> *"But thanks be to God, which giveth us the victory through our Lord Jesus Christ."* 1 Corinthians 15:57   God delivers on time.

10

God Healed My Broken Heart

⌘

God, the Supreme Creator and Ruler woke me up out of a spiritual sleep. He renewed my mind and spoke to my heart. The Holy Spirit reminded me of God's Sovereignty in predestination and ordination. Before the foundation of this world, God had chosen and ordained me for salvation, sanctification and service. He called me to be a blessing to others. *God delivers on time.*

The Holy Spirit reminded that God has prepared a place for His children.

"In my Father's house are many mansions; if it were not so I would have told you. I go to prepare a place for you." John 14:2

The Holy Spirit reminded that God has appointed once unto men to die, but after this the judgment.

"And as it is appointed unto men once to die, but after this

the judgment." Hebrews 9:27

The Holy Spirit reminded that God does not make mistakes in calling His children home to Paradise.

"Assuredly, I say to you, today you will be with me in paradise." Luke 23:43

The Holy Spirit reminded that God has removed His children from the evil to come. They are resting at peace in Paradise.

"1 The righteous perisheth, and no man layeth it to heart: and merciful men are taken away, none considering that the righteous is taken away from the evil to come." Isaiah 57:1

The Holy Spirit also reminded me that He had not given me a spirit of fear.

"For God hath not given us the spirit of fear; but of power, and of love, and of a sound mind." 2 Timothy 1:7

The Holy Spirit had reaffirmed God's Word and convicted my spirit. I cried to the Lord, and He my cry. Then, I repented. God healed my broken heart and restored the joy of my salvation on May 6, 2007. He later manifested healing in other areas of my body. I began to study and meditate on God's Word. I returned to church and publicly testified of what God had done for me. God has given us an opportunity to confess our sins of disobedience and repent of our ungodly ways. This action on our part breaks the bondage in our lives. *God delivers on time.*

Later, I was in an automobile accident that required two

surgeries. Then, my doctor diagnosed me with mass in both thyroid lobes and abnormal cells. There were times when I could not talk. My hair broke off. I even gained weight, and I started to regress emotionally. Reather had concerns about me regressing to a state of depression. She often said that I needed healing from Mother's passing. I also needed to relocate because I had gone through a lot and not everyone handled grief or tragedies in the same manner. At that moment, I was confused. I was not in denial. Mother's spirit was/is within me, and she would never leave me. Most importantly, along with Jesus, I would see her again. God knows what we need. He always knows what is best for His children; therefore, God gave me a desire to move. I begin to make preparations by downsizing to make life comfortable for me. Keesha located apartments on the North end of Lima for Raymond, her family, and I. In the meantime, my health was not improving, so I had a total throidectomy in Columbus, Ohio. The mass was benign, and my cells have returned to normal. My body is going through transitions because God created our organs for a purpose. After a surgical procedure to remove an organ from your body has occurred, medications will help; however, your body is never the same and cannot function at its fullest potential.

Some healing manifestations are miraculously instantaneous and others a process over time; nevertheless, God's Word heals, delivers, and restores. When the enemy tries to steal my healing or causes me to doubt, I quote the following scripture and other healing scriptures.

"4 Surely he hath borne our griefs, and carried our sorrows: yet we did esteem him stricken, smitten of God, and afflicted. 5 But he was wounded for our transgressions, he was bruised for our iniquities: the chastisement of our peace was upon him; and with his stripes we are healed." Isaiah 53:4-5

The good news is that in God's Kingdom (Utopia), deaths, suffering, pain, heartache, financial or economic crisis, affliction or problems of any kind will exist. *God delivers on time.*

Let us be mindful that no matter what we go through, God is sovereign. What does it mean to say that God is sovereign?

"God is God, He is the Most High, doing according to His will in the army of Heaven, and among the inhabitants of the earth, so that none can stay His hand or say unto Him "What doest Thou?" Daniel 4:35

"He is the Almighty, the Possessor of all power in Heaven and earth, so that none can defeat His counsels, thwart His purpose, or resist His will." Psalms 115:3

"He is "The Governor among the nations setting up kingdoms" overthrowing empires, and determining the course of dynasties as pleaseth Him best." Psalms 22:28

"He is the "Only Potentate, the King of kings, and Lord of lords" 1 Timothy 6:15: Such is the God of the Bible.

"God is the greatness, and the power, and the glory, and the

victory, and the majesty: for all that is in the heaven and in the earth is Thine; Thine is the kingdom, O LORD, and Thou art exalted as Head above all." 1 Chronicles 29:11 God delivers on time.

Jesus Christ, the only begotten Son of God has paid the price. According to *Isaiah 53:4-5,* Jesus Christ has redeemed us from sin, sickness, disease, poverty, family issue, and other mountains. We need to receive, apply God's Word to any situation, speak to the mountain (s), and wait on God. To receive is to take or accept something.

"Therefore I say unto you, What things so ever ye desire, when ye pray, believe that ye receive them, and ye shall have them." Mark 11: 23

God is working in His called lives for the good according to His purpose.

"And we know that all things work together for good to them that love God, to them who are the called according to his purpose." Romans 8:28

God healed my broken heart; however, I neglected to pray and meditate on God's Word, daily. As a result, my healing was unprotected, and I was unable to retain it.

It is vital for us to do what is necessary to maintain our healing and our faith. Protecting both is not an indication that God's Word is untrue. His Word is the same **yesterday, today** and **forever more**. Let us be mindful that Satan, the thief, comes to steal, kill, and destroy. *God delivers on time*

11

My Acceptance Process

My acceptance of Mother home going would release me to continue the work of the ministry; nevertheless, God was not through with me yet. I needed God's active Word in my life daily to maintain healing, deliverance, and to be a blessing to others. I had to go through my valley of the grief stages. The grief stages are denial and isolation, bargaining, anger, depression, and acceptance; however, each individual does not grieve in the same manner. *God delivers on time.*

God is good, all the time. God knows what we stand in need of and how to give us our breakthroughs. He knew that I needed a breakthrough because Satan would have destroyed me. God blessed me to move from the last home Mother and I shared on July 30, 2010; nevertheless, that transition was difficult for me. It felt as if I was leaving Mother and a part of me behind. I cried profusely because the acceptance process had begun. I thank the Holy Spirit and Sister Clara for comforting me. *God delivers on time.*

I did not know that writing this book would be a part of my healing process. I even had mixed emotions about sharing Mother's legacy with the world; however, I shared my thoughts with Tomika, Sister Moore, and James.

"Mom, this is what God and Granny would want you to do. Granny was a giver; she gave her life to the work of the ministry and blessed many. You are carrying her mantle now, so you have to share her with the world, while pursuing the work of her ministry," Tomika said.

"God saved, sanctified, baptized and filled Mother Wilson with His precious Holy Ghost for the work of the ministry. She preached God's Word. Then, God later birthed a healing, deliverance, and prophetic ministries through her, and she was a blessing to others. Before her spirit returned to the presence of God, she imparted the mantle to you to carry on the work of the ministry in her absence. Her final destination of certainty is Heaven (Utopia).

Apostle Paul wrote most of the New Testament, and God blessed us through his writing. You have written about Mother's legacy. Releasing her anointing through your writing will enable God to bless others as well as your self. Healing will manifest in your body, and you will feel better to continue the work of the ministry. In the meantime, your book is destined go places where you cannot," Sister Moore said.

"At least you recognize where you are because most people do not, " James said.

God, Tomika and Sister Jean Moore reaffirmed my calling. James reminded me that my emotions are normal because I am human. I appreciate their input. I later shared my experience with Keesha, and she was happy for me. *God delivers on time.*

God through my writing has helped me to release Mother mentally and place her home going in the right prospective. When God calls our spirit into His presence, no cemetery will discriminate. The grave accepts all ages, sizes, race, family members, friends, brothers and sisters in Christ, unwell, etc. In the meantime, God designed grieving to be a healthy process; nevertheless, daily grieving will cause a spirit of grief to manifest, resulting in sickness and disease.

The saints were correct in their encouragement. Mother was in a better place. She would not want me to grieve for nearly two years, but accept God's divine will for her home going. She wanted us to give God the glory, honor, and praise for what He had done. On the other hand, she knew that I would cry sometimes; nevertheless, God would heal my broken heart and release me to move forward. The Holy Spirit would comfort me. Most importantly, Jesus Christ would never leave or forsaken me. I would then mature spiritually and become stronger in my walk in Christ to continue the work of the ministry to be a blessing to others.

When someone we love dies, even the elderly, we grieve. We should also honor the positive impact they had in our lives and in this world. For some who find it difficult to believe in the afterlife, it can be a very sad time, presuming that the departed have dissipated out of life, never to be seen again. Allow your emotions to flow through the stages of grief. Then, God will heal your broken hearts, and the Holy Ghost will comfort you. Most importantly, God's Word is essential in moving us forward in Christ. When I occasionally cry for Mother, not grieve, the Holy Spirit comforts me with God's Word:

"16 For the Lord himself shall descend from heaven with a shout, with the voice of the archangel, and with the trump of God: and the dead in Christ shall rise first: 17 Then we which are alive and remain shall be caught up together with them in the clouds, to meet the Lord in the air: and so shall we ever be with the Lord.18 Wherefore comfort one another with these words."
1 Thessalonians 4:16-18

Other grieving scriptures are found in the following books: Psalm 23;4: Psalm 119;50: Isaiah 41;10: Isaiah 43;2: Isaiah 49;13: Isaiah 51;11:1 Corinthians 15;55-57: 2 Corinthians 1;3-4:2 Corinthians 5;8: 1Thessalonians 4:;13-14: 2 Thessalonians 2;16-17: Hebrews 4;15-16:1 Peter 5;7: Revelation 21;4.

God has healed, delivered, and released me, and my stages of grief is complete. God has given me a peace that passeth all understanding.

MY ACCEPTANCE PROCESS

7 And the peace of God, which passeth all understanding, shall keep your hearts and minds through Christ Jesus." Philippians 4:7   God delivers on time.

God's children are on a journey; nevertheless, we will go through trials. Trail is a test or experiment to determine the quality, safety, performance, usefulness, or public acceptance of something. Additionally, a trial is an instance of trouble or hardship, especially one that tests somebody's ability to endure.

"7 That the trial of your faith, being much more precious than of gold that perisheth, though it be tried with fire, might be found unto praise and honour and glory at the appearing of Jesus Christ" 1 Peter 1:7.

God's children will go through tribulations. Tribulation is hardship or a cause of suffering.

"3 And not only so, but we glory in tribulations also: knowing that tribulation worketh patience; 4 And patience, experience; and experience, hope: 5 And hope maketh not ashamed; because the love of God is shed abroad in our hearts by the Holy Ghost which is given unto us." Romans 5:3-5

God's children will suffer infirmities in our flesh, just like the Apostle Paul did. His throne in the flesh was a messenger from Satan to buffer him. He was not sick. In your Bible Dictionary, infirmity is hardship, stress etc. In your regular dictionary it is a lack of strength, character flaw, and minor illness; nevertheless, our spiritual promotion will take us to the next stage. To suffer is to feel pain, undergo something unpleasant, endure something, and have a weakness or illness…

God's children will suffer afflictions, just as Paul did. Affliction is a condition of great physical or mental distress. Continued afflictions could cause sickness and disease to come upon us, but God will deliver us out of them all.

"19 Many are the afflictions of the righteous: but the LORD delivereth him out of them all." Psalms 34:19

God's children will suffer persecution, just like the Apostle Paul did. The truth is that God did not redeem us from persecution. Persecution is the subjecting of a race or group of people to cruel or unfair treatment, e.g. because of their ethnic origin or religious beliefs.

"Yea and all that will live godly in Christ Jesus shall suffer persecution." 2 Timothy 3:12

God's children will suffer a while; however, we will receive God's benefits.

"But the God of all grace, who hath called us unto his eternal glory by Christ Jesus, after that ye have suffered a while, make you perfect, stablish, strengthen, settle you." 1 peter 5: 10

God's children will suffer; nevertheless, we are destined to reign with Christ.

"If we suffer, we shall also reign with him: if we deny him, he also will deny us:" 2 Timothy 2:12

God's children must remain prayerful, study God's Word, do not fret or give up. What we think is a problem could be our miracle. What we think is a test, is our testimony. What we think is a mess, is our message. What we think is a lie on us, is life to us. What we rebuke, God has not removed from us because in it is a purging for us. No matter what we go through, God's grace is sufficient for all. Grace is a gift from God to humankind, favor...

"9 And he said unto me, My grace is sufficient for thee: for my strength is made perfect in weakness. Most gladly therefore will I rather glory in my infirmities, that the power of Christ may rest upon me" 2 Corinthians 12:9.   God delivers on time.

God's children must put on the whole Armor of God *(His* Word) in preparation for the gospel of peace.

"14 Stand therefore, having your loins girt about with truth, and having on the breastplate of righteousness; 15 And your feet shod with the preparation of the gospel of peace;16 Above all, taking the shield of faith, wherewith ye shall be able to quench all the fiery darts of the wicked. 17 And take the helmet of salvation, and the sword of the Spirit, which is the word of God: 18 Praying always with all prayer and supplication in the Spirit, and watching thereunto with all perseverance and supplication for all saints;" Ephesians 6:14-18

I thank God for blessing me to go through the grieving stages. I thank God for divine revelation relating to the death realm for His children. I thank God for giving me the courage to shop again at Mother's favorite store Wal-Mart Shopping Center and eat at her favorite restaurants, Golden Corral and Cracker Barrel Old Country

Store, Inc. I also thank God for releasing me to continue the work of the ministry in Mother's absence. For additional information about the stages of grief, go to www.stagesofgrief.com. *God delivers on time.*

12

My Memories

My memories of Mother are great. She was comical and so am I. We are God's Children, and He is also humorous. Laughter is like a medicine to our soul. It will enable us to heal and maintain our healing. God delivers on time.

Mother was in my life for 53 years. We shared a special bond. No earthly human could ever replace her; show me her love, compassion, kindness, patience, discipline, understanding, or consideration. She has crossed over; however, her spirit resides within me. We are still a part of each other. Today, I think of her as my assigned guardian angel.

I remember talking with Mother on the telephone daily before we moved in together. If I did not call her first, she called me.

"I hadn't heard from you today. You have put me in the trash can and covered me up," she would say.

Mother and I attended church and enjoyed watching God work. Her healing and deliverance ministries always amazed me.

Mother always reminded her children to either set the clock up or back. One Sunday at church, I wondered why our deacons had already taken the tithes and offerings up. Then, I noticed the clock was one hour later and thought that maybe it needed repair.

Later, Beverly revealed to me that the time had been set-up. I realized then what I had taken for granted was now important.

I remember when Mothers' out of state children vacationed with us. We had fun eating out, shopping and taking pictures. We looked forward to seeing them come to Lima.

Mother always called her children to sing happy birthday. She would use the highest musical note at the end singing, "you, you, and you!" She always made our day. Before she passed, she called Brother Arthur Knuckles and sang, Happy Birthday, to him, and that made his day. Today, I am continuing her trend by calling our family. However, I cannot sing it like Mother did.

I remembered being Mother's cosmetologist. One evening she insisted that I do her hair. I was exhausted; nevertheless, I wanted to please her. I premed her hair and mistakenly used holding spray to roll her hair instead of setting lotion. Consequently, her hair was stiff as a board. I was too tired to rinse and reset it. Desiring not to hear her reaction, I quickly left her apartment and drove home. The following morning she called and mentioned how hard and stiff her hair was. She could not sleep without doing a rinse out. I mentioned what I had done wrong, and we laughed. Later, that day I rinsed and reset her hair, using setting lotion this time.

I remembered driving Mother and Sister Clara to a restaurant for supper. Suddenly, I forgot where we were going and drove us to the mall. I guess my mind was on shopping.

"Jackie, are you all right? Why are we at the mall and not the restaurant?" Mother asked.

"I forgot where I was going, mom. Shoot, I am tired."

She finally recognized that I was fatigued and needed to go home. She quickly suggested a carry out. I am sure that she was praying for me. Lesson learned; one should never do anything while exhausted because mistakes are more likely to happen.

I remember Mother experiencing fake fingernails, and she glued her fingers together. Wow, we had fun that day. I started to tease her by saying the glue was there permanently, but changed my mind. She would have wanted to fast and pray for my deliverance (again). Her nurse at the Elderly Day Center told me that she did not glue her nails on correctly and lost a few. My Mother was not going out like that, so I secured her nails. *God delivers on time.*

I remember God blessing Mother with a Craftmatic

twin bed and a lift chair. She made it clear that I was not to sit on either one as I might damage the motors. I did not realize that I was overweight. I guess mom saw something I did not because she later purchased me an exercise bike.

I remember wondering why Mother's lift chair was remaining in an upright position. She told me it was stuck, but that the technician was coming to fix it. Another time, I noticed her bed was stuck in the same position. Again, the technician was coming to fix it. Thankfully, he was able to repair them both. She never showed discouragement about her chair or bed's dysfunctions. Once victory had manifested itself in any situation she encountered, she would say, "Now take that Mr. Devil!" I was happy not to have been responsible for those dysfunctions.

I remember Mother's last Easter with Charles, Keesha, and their family. We worshipped with them at their church. She danced for the Lord because He had blessed her. Keesha invited us for dinner. Later, Tomika and her family joined us. We ate, took numerous pictures and had a glorious time.

I remember holiday seasons with Mother being joyous occasions. We ate, listened to gospel comedy and music, told jokes, laughed, took pictures, opened and exchanged gifts. Today I cherish those memories.

I remember us shopping at a local store. She purchased two bags of pork skins. I busted Mother because neither of us was supposed to be eating pork; however, those skins smelled so good. I grabbed her bag and had a serious relapse. We ate both bags in the parking lot. Minutes later, I felt lightheaded and ill. My blood pressure had elevated. I could not drive us home, and Mother noticed.

"Jackie, what's wrong. Are you alright?"

Mother finally realized that I could not speak, anointed me with oil, and prayed. Gods' healing power manifested, and I drove us home. God hears a Mother's prayer. Most importantly, the effectual fervent prayer of a righteous man availeth much.

"Confess your faults one to another, and pray one for another, that ye may be healed. The effectual fervent prayer of a righteous man availeth much." James 5: 16

I remember driving past a local store that sold country ham and mentioned my desire to Mother.

"Yeah, let's buy some good old country ham. I haven't had country ham in years," Mother said.

I remembered getting deadly ill when I relapsed with mom before, so I refused to stop at the store.

"Oh no mom, I am not getting sick today, my dear. The reason you did not get sick before was because your system was never cleanse of pork." I said.

The only regret that I have is not allowing her to eat country ham. Her spirit was soon to enter Paradise anyway, so that should not have mattered. Well, my intention was good. In the meantime, do all that you can for your loved ones; God will bless you.

I remember asking Mother why she kept torn stockings.

"I can wear them underneath my pants and no one will know," she replied.

"I hope you'll never have an emergency."

"Jackie, no one has business underneath my clothes without a reason. I am not worried. Why are you?" she asked.

I remember visiting Mother in Lenoir, North Carolina. I saw a lizard in her front yard and ran screaming into her house. She thought I had lost my natural mind because I lived with lizards and snakes all of my life. At that time, that did not matter because I had lived in Lima, Ohio for over 20 years. Before she returned to Lima, she mentioned that a lizard had gotten in her apartment, and she and Raymond ran outdoors. I could not believe what I had just heard. She could be afraid of lizards, but I could not. Something was wrong with that picture. I reminded her of what she had told me about being fearful of lizards.

"Yes, but I never saw one in my house before," she replied.

I remember us watching our last movie Home Alone. In the beginning, she expressed her opinions.

"Jackie, that boy is bad. He needs his behind whipped."

"Mom, just watch the movie and see what happens."

"I don't care. I have never seen a kid so bad."

"Mom, please be quiet."

Before the movie had ended, she was laughing. She enjoyed that movie. She realized that Kevin was a hero for his family.

I remember us thinking that large snails were in our yard. I never liked worms, snakes, snails, or any earthy crickets, although, God created them for a reason. I poured a box of salt on them, hoping they would melt, and we left home. After our return, we noticed they had crawled over the salt and onto our front storm door. Mother had a shocking look on her face, but she dared to respond. I screamed so loudly that I frightened her.

"Shut up, Jackie. Those snails will not harm you!" My brave mother screamed.

The next day, we noticed snails were still in our yard, so I called a local store. While talking with one of their representatives, he laughed at me. He then informed me that they were not snails but sluggers, as if I was supposed to have known that. Mother and I drove there and purchased a product to remove them.

I remember Mother having a not so good moment, and I called Inez. She would tease mom about coming to Lima in her helicopter. Inez always made her day.

One cold winter day, Sister Clara accompanied me to view Mother's gravesite. As we were walking up that long steep cold icy hill, she made a statement about Mother that caused us to laugh. I had not laughed that hard since her home going.

"Mother knows how to get us to exercise, doesn't she? One day she will burst out of that grave. The Bible says the dead in Christ shall rise first... I can see Mother now with her hand on her hip."

"What do you mean a hand on her hip? Mother's spirit would have been in God's presence. Do you actually believe she will have just one hand on her hip? I think both hands will be on her hips," I happily stated.

Today, Todochi and I place flowers in a vase on Mother's gravesite because she loved roses and plants. She had a green thumb, but I can kill any plant without trying.

Mother Wilson has left us a legacy. Her journey included a ministry of motherhood, and she was a blessing to others. God sent our spirits to earth through parents of His choice for His plan and purpose. We did not choose our biological parents. God chose Ms. Sarah Wilson to be the mother of six children, including Samuel, Inez, Isaiah, Boyd, Raymond, and myself. She had 21 grandchildren, 27 great-grandchildren, and 1 great, great-grandchild. He also blessed her with two goddaughters, Sister Clara White and Ms. Emma McNeal, a godson Mr. Curtis knuckles, and many brothers and sisters in Christ. She loved us unconditionally, and we loved her. She gave us flowers while she lived, and we gave hers to see and smell.

It is crucial that we honor our parents, regardless of unfortunate past or present situations. Being pregnant, giving birth and rearing us should be reasons enough to honor them. Mother and I had our moments; nevertheless, I would never intentionally dishonor her. Sometimes we acted like biological sisters, having our differences but never serious enough to divide us. If I forgot my place as her daughter, she quickly reminded me. If someone dishonored her, we quickly reminded him or her. There are serious consequences when you dishonor your parents.

"2 Honour thy father and mother; (which is the first commandment with promise;) 3That it may be well with thee, and thou mayest live long on the earth." Ephesians 6: 2-3

Since Mothers passing, our family's relationship is stronger. Inez and I now have a special bond similar to that shared by Mother and Aunt Louise. We talk weekly. Reather, my cousin and I talk almost daily. My other siblings and I also talk frequently. Raymond has returned to Lima Ohio to be near me. Clyde Jr. always called daily and spoke with his grandma and I. He continues to call me, and we have great conversations. Today I intercede for my family and others, just like Mother did. I feel like their mother now. The last is first and the first last.

I thank God for choosing Ms. Sarah Mae Wilson to be our mother. Today, I have great memories of her time spent here with me, and I will cherish them forever. We all loved Mother Wilson, but God loved her best.

Laughter is like a medicine. Try laughing daily; it releases stress that causes sickness and disease.

"A merry heart doeth good like a medicine: but a broken spirit drieth the bones." Proverbs 17:22   *God delivers on time.*

13

History to Achieving Our Goals

Our history is crucial because knowledge is power and freedom; however, if misused, you will find yourself in bondage again. Allow me to share my history with you. *God delivers on time.*

My grandparents Mr. & Mrs. Forest and Amanda Littlejohn Branan's union produced three children including Sarah, Louise, and Grover Branan. Our mother Sarah was born on August 19, 1923. She was intelligent, an excellent student. She represented her school in the Spelling Bee contests and each time, she won first place. She brought trophies and ribbons home to her school. Later, my grandparents divorced and then he passed. My grandma remarried Rev. Herbert Borders. They were homeowners, farmers, and sharecroppers. They modernized our home. They were responsible for us having indoor running water, a bathroom, and a wringer washing machine. They also had a washhouse built to do laundry in.

Mr. & Mrs. Clarence and Sarah (our mother) Wilson's union produced two children including Samuel and Inez. They later divorced. Mother and her children returned home to her parents. She later birthed four more children including Isaiah, Boyd, Raymond and I, which was a part of God's plan. At that time, she was unaware of child support and struggled to make ends meet. She and grandma worked hard to maintain our home. They picked cotton and people hired them to wash and iron their clothes. In the meantime, Mother was dissatisfied with their line of work. She believed that God had more to offer them. She sought for better employment and worked two domestic jobs that changed the course of our lifestyle forever. She was the accountant in our home. Grandma stopped gardening, raising cattle, working the fields, and doing other people's laundry.

Mother advanced our living standard. She bought a new electric stove, refrigerator, and kerosene heaters. They started to buy groceries from the marketplace, which was different. She learned to cook with different seasonings including bay leaves, oregano, garlic, basil etc. The taste of our food greatly improved and was never the same. She learned to bake red velvet, lemon and orange glaze cakes, which was different. We were used to chocolate, vanilla and pound cakes. Mother taught grandma advanced cooking skills, and they were the Chefs in our home. She purchased an electric sewing machine to improve their sewing skills. She was the tailor for many in our neighborhood, including us. Most store-bought items did not fit perfectly; therefore, she was creative in making them fit. She learned how to knit, crochet, quilt, and needle point. She increased her income by selling some of her crafts. *God delivers on time.*

God had blessed Mother to be a blessing to our family and others; nevertheless, she knew that education would result to security and freedom. Her desire was that she and her children obtain a high school diploma and further our education. She never wanted us to struggle, but have a good life. She prayed, worked hard and supported her family. Then, God granted her desire. Samuel, Isaiah and Boyd graduated from Douglas High School. Samuel and Isaiah continued their education. The city employed Boyd, but he later passed. Inez, Raymond and I would eventually achieve our goals. *God delivers on time.*

When God bless us, Satan comes to steal our joy; he wants our strength. I was 12 years old when Mother's trials and tribulations began. Our doctor diagnosed her with a heart condition without hope of recovery. She could not walk, talk and was bedridden. She had no money to support us; nevertheless, God was preparing her for the work of the ministry. He would also teach her how to trust Him. Our grandparents supported us without grumbling, and we never wanted for anything. Following three years of sickness, Mother had past the test. God birthed a healing, deliverance and prophetic ministries through her with an increased anointing to bless others. She committed her life to God, the highest authority and willingly served Him. My life was never the same. I was/am a preachers' granddaughter. Now, I was/am a preacher's kid (PK) which was difficult for me. I was around mostly ministers whose standards were very high. They did not allow me to go to many places and wear certain apparels because it was sinful. At one time, Mother and I listened and studied God's Word on cassette tapes. We also studied God's Word through Bible Correspondence Schools and received certificates. She and grandpa taught me how to play the piano. At one time, I was a pianist and drummer for our church. Today, I am thankful for having a God-fearing Mother. Her biblical fundamental teachings caused me to be who I am today in Christ. *God delivers on time.*

After Mother's restoration, God opened the windows of Heaven for her. Her season of blessings had come. Southern Desk Furniture in Hickory, North Carolina employed her as an inspector, where she worked for five years. During that period, she got her driver license and bought a car. Later, she and I moved there, so she could be closer to her job. The transitional process was difficulty for me. I wanted to stay with my grandparents because they were my safety zone. I cried; however, grandma Mrs. Amanda Borders helped me to let go. Her doctor later diagnosed her with leukemia. At that time, I was unemployed, so I moved back home and became her caregiver. Later, God's angel carried her spirit to the presence of God in Paradise on June 1, 1971. Her spirit also settled in our hearts.

Mother purchased a new house in Newton, North Carolina. Unfortunately, her employer laid her off. She did not fret because her faith was in God, and she was assertive. She sought for another employment. Newton City Schools employed her as Head of the Custodian Department. I married, and we later moved to Ohio. Later, God's angel carried my grandpa Rev. Herbert Borders spirit to the presence of God in Paradise on June 30, 1976. His spirit also settled in our hearts.

During Mother's employment, my grandparents played major roles in my life. After they passed, my life was never the same. Today, I am thankful for having God-fearing grandparents in my life. Their biblical fundamental teachings caused me to also be who I am today in Christ. *God delivers on time.* .

Mother later retired, registered her home on the market, and move to Ohio. There, God had a work for her to do. Later, our doctor diagnosed her twice with cancer. She faced the death angel, but each time, God healed and delivered her with an increased anointing to continue the work of the ministry. *God delivers on time.*

Mother had encountered many adversities; nevertheless, God highly favored and blessed her to graduate at age 80. She received her high school diploma and class ring on July 30, 2004. She also received a Preliminary Certificate from the Commonwealth of Pennsylvania Department of Education. Prior to her 2004 accomplishment, she received her: Ordination License through Unity Holy Church Of God, a Certificate of Ministry through United Christian Church & Ministerial Associations, Inc., a Certificate in Pastoral Training at Liberty Temple Church, Diploma from the Voice Of Prophecy-Worldwide Bible Broadcasters-New Life Bible Correspondence School, Certificates for Floral Design and Forklift Operator, just to name a few. Mother was also the founder for the, "Prayer Room For All People" in Lenoir, North Carolina. She was there for five years, and God used her to bless others. We were proud of Mother's accomplishments.

Inez and I achieved our goals of graduating, receiving our high school diplomas and class rings with honor to our Lord and Savior, Jesus Christ in 2004. We received Preliminary Education Certificates from the Commonwealth of Pennsylvania Department of education. We also felt better about ourselves. Afterward, I believed that nothing could stop me from attaining any goal I wanted to achieve. I am continuing my education in the medical field and Theology. Our brother Raymond is enrolling in school to obtain his high school diploma and class ring. Then, Mother's desires would have happen

God brought Mother from, through, and over many trials and tribulations, and she past the test. Then, God heavily anointed her for the work of the ministry to be a blessing to others. She was wiser, educated, and felt better about herself. If we do not pass the test, we will retake it. Sometimes, the examination gets harder because Satan does not want us to mature spiritually. G*od delivers on time*

Our Mother has left us a legacy. She established a spiritual foundation, morals and work ethics for her family. Her Ministry took her extensively throughout the United States, and she was a blessing to many. *God delivers on time.*

Our history is vital because it gives direction for our futures. I thank God for Mother instilling into us that prayer, hard work, education, patience, determination, remaining focused and striving for the best would enable us to achieve our goals. Most importantly, do your best and God will do the rest. *God delivers on time.*

14

In the Midst of Our Storms

In the midst of our storms, the Lord's great power will manifest and have its way. Storm is a strong rain, wind, thunder, snow etc, any heavy fall of snow, rain, etc, a strong emotional outburst, or a sudden disturbance. A storm can be symbolic of an obstacle, hindrance, or insurmountionable problem. Each season has its storm because we are in spiritual warfare. We have crosses to bear, as Jesus did. When we are going through a storm, sometimes, before leaving it, another one began. Satan is tempting us to bring out the bad. God is allowing adversities to bring out the good. God always has His way in the midst of our storms.

"The LORD is slow to anger, and great in power, and will not at all acquit (not guilty) the wicked: the LORD hath his way in the whirlwind and in the storm, and the clouds are the dust of his feet." Nahum 1: 3   God delivers on time.

God will bless you in the midst of your storms. God has brought me through and over many storms, and He blessed me to be a blessing to others. Allow me to share my blessings for your encouragement. God extended my family because children are a blessing from Him. I have another grandson, Johnavin Smith (JJ), Charles and Keesha's son on September 28, 2006. She finally had the boy she had always wanted. God blessed me with my first great-grandson, Derrick Jackson Jr. (DJ), Derrick Sr and Sakeyna's son on November 20, 2006. I have another granddaughter, Gabrielle Mae Wells, (Miracle), Todochi's daughter on January 7, 2008. She has Mother's middle name, "Mae."

God blessed me to complete my education. I received a certificate from Penn Foster Career School in Medical Coding and Billing on January 8, 2009. I received a certificate of completion in Theology from the Herbert W. Armstrong Bible College and Correspondence School on June 23, 2010. I would like to give special thanks to Dr. Melvin Monroe and his staff for assisting me with letters, so I could continue my education. I also would like to thank him for encouraging me during the bereavement of Mother. *God delivers on time*

My daughter Keesha is a State Tested Nursing Assistant (STNA). My daughter Tomika graduated from North Central State College on August 31, 2010. The Ohio State Board of Nursing granted her a Practical Nurse-M-1V certificate on November 10, 2010. She intends to further

her education in the medical field. My son Todochi is concentrating on getting his Master Degree at Bowling Green University. My granddaughter Sakeyna graduated from Lima Senior High School, where she attended Multiple Intelligence. She is a State Tested Nursing Assistant (STNA). My granddaughter TaQuayla graduated from Perry High School. She attended Apollo Career Center, where she received an Administrative Assistant and a State Tested Nursing Assistant Certificates (STNA). She is currently attending Rhodes State College, concentrating in Physical Therapy. I am proud of their accomplishments. What Satan meant for evil, God turned for our good. Mother would say, "Now take that Mr. Devil."

I thank God for having His way in the midst of my storms. God will bless you in the midst of yours. God always have His way in the midst of our storms because He is not through with us yet.

"The LORD is slow to anger, and great in power, and will not at all acquit (not guilty) the wicked: the LORD hath his way in the whirlwind and in the storm, and the clouds are the dust of his feet." Nahum 1: 3   God delivers on time.

15

America's Destiny

God is the Supreme Creator and Ruler over all things. Based on God foreknowledge and His divine declaration, God chose the United States of America's destiny. His primary divine purpose was/is for us to fulfill His plan of salvation and be a blessing to other nations as well as our own. *God delvers on time.*

Allow me to refresh your memory: Senator Barack Obama graduated from Harvard Law School, worked as a community organizer, civil rights attorney, and law professor, just to name a few. He is married to Michelle Obama, who is also an attorney. They have two daughters Malia and Sasha. As a candidate for President, I believe that he understands America's crises are real, serious, and many. Our economy has weakened; homes, jobs and businesses have been lost. Our healthcare is too costly and out of control. Too many of our schools and colleges have failed. We are involved in two wars. We also have not accepted responsibility for our choices and consequences of our actions. During his campaign, he laid out a vision to end the war in Iraq responsibly and bring our troops home. He plans to reform healthcare, so everyone can have medical insurance. He plans to reform our schools and colleges, so our students can compete with today's world. He plans to restore our work force and the economy, just to name a few. His pledge to the American people was a defining part of his vision. His vision was one of the reasons that all of us knocked on doors, made phone calls, and voted.

God moved beyond all racial barriers and decreed a historic moment on November 5, 2008. Our character was not judged by our skin tone. We finally realized that fighting amongst ourselves was not accomplishing anything. We recognized that failure is the result of division. The minority helped the majority fulfill God's Perfect Will and not ours. The people elected Senator Barack Obama for President of the United States of America. His campaign speech was spiritual and awesome. It was as if Dr. Martin Luther King Jr's voice was speaking through his essentially saying, "I Have A Dream." Dr. King's prophecy from God was no longer a dream, but a reality. I remembered his wife Mrs. Coretta King, as well as Malcolm X, Adam C. Powell, Rosa Park, Ralph Abernathy, Andrew Young, Rev Jesse Jackson, just to name a few, who prayed, marched and/or died to make this great day possible. I also recalled Lyndon B. Johnson, John F. Kennedy, Robert Kennedy, Ted Kennedy, and other politicians who supported the Civil Rights movement.

I believe other African-Americans were overwhelmed with joy. We definitely have no more excuses. I called family and friends rejoicing in what God had done. I wished Mother and other deceased family members were here to celebrate this event. Mother would have praised God to the highest. President-Elect Obama's parents and grandparents passed before this great day transpired. They would have been proud of his accomplishment. Let us be mindful that when imagination joins common purpose, goals and achievements will result. I was excited because this victory has given me a new outlook on life and hope for our future. I know that with God all things are possible.

"But Jesus beheld them, and said unto them, With men this is impossible; but with God all things are possible." Matthew 19:25-26 God delvers on time.

America's destiny manifested with the inauguration for President-Elect Barrack Obama on January 20, 2009. At 9:45 AM, the Obama's attend a private prayer service held at the St. John Cathedral (church of the presidents) located near the White House in Washington, D.C. Bishop T.D. Jakes ministered on Daniel being in the Lion's Den. He realized the challenges America is facing, and only God can bring about the change we need. Later, the Obama's met with President George W. Bush and *first lady,* Barbara Bush for private coffee. He was thankful to former President Bush for the generosity he showed throughout the transition process to the White House.

The inaugural ceremony began at 10:15 AM. Mrs. Michelle Obama and their daughters, including Malia and Sasha were dressed for the occasion. Millions of people including Democrats, Republicans, other politicians, blacks, whites, and other cultures attended the ceremony. The Queen of Music Aretha Franklin sang at the great event. The weather was extremely cold with subzero temperature and snow, but it did not matter. God was in charge. He was in the midst.

I praised God for allowing me to see this great day. At noon, President-Elect Barrack Obama was sworn in as the 44th President of the United States of America. Mrs. Michelle Obama is now *first lady* of our nation. His inauguration address (speech) presented on Capitol Hill was again awesome, and we will never forget that moment. He was humbled by the task before him, grateful for the trust we had bestowed on him, and mindful of the sacrifices born by our ancestors. Let us be mindful of what our ancestors did to build this great nation. Additionally, what they went through for our freedom. Slaves built the White House. They worked hard, fought, and many died. Our ancestor's ideas maybe considered old, but they are still true.

Some question President Obama's abilities and skills to lead America. God chose President Obama for such a time and season as this. God ordained ministers and placed them in authority, but for the good.

"1 For there is no power but of God: the powers that be are ordained of God. 2 Whosoever therefore resisteth the power resisteth the ordinance of God: and they that resist shall receive to themselves damnation. 3 For rulers are not a terror to good works, but to the evil. Wilt thou then not be afraid of the power? do that which is good, and thou shalt have praise of the same: 4 For he is the minister of God to thee for good. But if thou do that which is evil, be afraid; for he beareth not the sword in vain: for he is the minister of God, a revenger to execute wrath upon him that doeth evil. 5 Wherefore ye must needs be subject, not only for wrath, but also for conscience sake. 6 for this cause pay ye tribute also: for they are God's ministers, attending continually upon this very thing." Romans 13:1-6

God has made us Kings and Priests unto Him.

"And hath made us Kings and Priests unto God and his Father; to him be glory and dominion for ever and ever. Amen'." Revelation 1: 6

President Obama's life was not easy. He worked hard to overcome oppression to rise to the highest office in the land; however, he never gave up. God will bless him to do what is best for the good of our nation; however, we should not expect him to solve problems overnight. Democrats and Republicans will differ; nevertheless, both parties have good ideas to bring to our nation. We need to stop pointing fingers, set aside our differences and stop fighting amongst each other. We need to work together by focusing on what is best for the good of our nation. God has called upon us to reshape and remake what seems to be an uncertain destiny. Now, let us reaffirm God's given promise that all men are equal and free by keeping our eyes on the horizon with God's grace upon us. We will pursue our fullest potential and measure happiness because greatness is not a gift it is earned. We, the people will carry forth the great gift of freedom and deliver it safely to future generations.

President Obama replaced fear with hope and unity of purpose. With his leading the way, we, the people supported his ideas, and we did it. He announced a plan to bring our Combat Brigades home from Iraq in February 2009. He ordered the evacuation of our military while redoubling our efforts to strengthen Iraqis' Security Forces, support their government and people. Last summer, nearly 100,000 U.S troops pulled out of Iraq with hopes for completion by 2011. Our nation's financial crisis was the worst this country has faced since the Great Depression. Nevertheless, this Congress passed the largest set of tax cuts for the middle class since President Reagan, the largest education reform since President Johnson, the largest infrastructure investment since President Eisenhower, and the largest clean-energy bill ever. Now -- even though we still have a ways to go -- the economy is growing again.

Prior to this Congress, lawmakers had talked about reforming health care for almost a century, but that never happened. We reformed the health care system. Now 32 million more Americans will have access to health coverage. They passed a new law to rein in the abuses on Wall Street and protect consumers. They passed the Recovery Act to get our economy growing again. We repealed "Don't Ask, Don't Tell" and ratified the START arms control treaty. We struck down that law and made this country a more just place.

The final week of 2010 wrapped up the 111th Congress, and today's post details (10) Democratic accomplishments during the last two years that you may not have known about. In spite of our nations' many challenges, Congress passed hundreds of bills, and President Obama issued numerous measures to improve the lives of millions of people and move our country forward. The list below is far from comprehension. Instead, it is a sampling of the many Democratic initiative enacted and set in motion during this Congress. These Acts are not in any particular order.

President Obama passed (1) the Family Smoking Prevention and Tobacco Control Act: To protects public health and prohibits tobacco companies from targeting children. (2) The creation of, Solar Energy Zones: The Interior and Energy Departments identified suitable 'solar energy zones' on public lands that will help move America toward greater energy innovation and independence. (3) The Veteran's Benefit Act of 2010: Improves employment opportunities for veterans, prevent homelessness, ensures the well-being of veterans and their families, and honor fallen service members and more. (4) The Food Safety Modernization Act: Overhauls America's food safety system to help endure consumers is not at risk. (5) The Small Business Jobs Act: Promotes job creation and spurs private sector growth. (6) The Edward M. Kennedy Serve America Act: Expands national service programs and encourages more Americans to get involved in their communities. (7) The Human Rights Enforcement Act: Helps enforce human rights laws and improve existing laws regarding genocide and child soldier recruitment. (8) The Race to the Top Education Reform: Raises education and achievement standards through local and inter-state competition, improves teacher accountability, encourage the "best practices" supports innovative data systems, and more. (9) The Healthy, Hunger-Free Kids Act: Improves standards for meal nutrition in schools and aim to reduce child obesity and hunger. (10) Hiring Incentives To Restore Employment (HIRE) Act: Cut taxes for companies that hire employees who have been job haunting for 60 days or more. In addition, to learn more about the local impact of Democrats' initiative in your state and community, you can visit organizing for America.com and click on PROGRESS.

President Barack Obama was/is facing challenges with courage and resolve. He never claimed that he could perform miracles; nevertheless, he is doing a great job. I thank God for uniting and giving us the desire to fulfill God's divine plan and purpose in choosing Senator Barrack Obama as our 44th President of United States of America. I believe that God will help him to accomplish goals He set before him, but in a timely manner. Our confidence must remain in God and not ourselves. In Christ, we can do all things through Christ, which strengthens us. It is vital that we keep President Barack Obama, *first lady* Michelle Obama and family, his administration, Democrats and Republican parties in prayer for God's protection, direction and guidance.

America's destiny continues; however, we need God's grace and mercy bestowed continuously upon us. God bless the United States of America, but America should bless God. *God delivers on time.*

16

America Combat Mission Ends in Iraq

President Obama marked the end of America's combat mission in Iraq on August 31, 2010. Ending this war mark a milestone in our nation's history. Even at a time of great uncertainty, our brave troops remind us that our future is in our own hands and that our best days are ahead. *God delivers on time.*

America's last combat brigade unit in Iraq, (the Army's Fourth Stryker Brigade) journeyed home in the pre-dawn darkness. Thousands of troops and hundreds of vehicles departed from Baghdad, passing through Kuwait in the early morning hours. For over seven years, American troops and coalition forces fought their way across similar highways, but this time, no shots were fired. It was just a convoy of brave Americans, making their way home.

All me to refresh your memory: Following 9-11, America bombed Iraq, and we were overwhelmed. Our troops embarked on a journey of the unknown in a foreign land. Their mission was as complex as any our military ever asked to face. People were killing anyone who represented good. A war to disarm a state became a fight against insurgency. Terrorism and sectarian warfare was tarring Iraq apart. The military had not properly trained our troops in disarming Improvised Explosive Device (I.E.D) roadside bombs; therefore, they were dying daily and others were injured. America persevered because of a belief we shared with the Iraqi people: A belief that out of the ashes of war, a new beginning could be born in this cradle of civilization. In an age without surrender ceremonies, we earned victory through the success of our forces and the strength of our own nation.

Every American who served joins an unbroken line of heroes that stretches from Lexington to Gettysburg; from Iwo Jima to Inchon; and from Khe m Sanh to Kandahar because they have fought to see that the life's of our children are better than our own. They confronted every challenge including defeated a regime that had terrorized the Iraqi people, closed or turned over to Iraq hundreds of our bases, and moved millions of pieces of equipment out of Iraq. They stared into the darkest of human creations, war. They fought in a faraway place for people they never knew. Many served multiple tours of duty, far from families who bore a heroic burden of their own, enduring the absence of a husband's embrace or a mother's kiss. Nearly 1.5 million Americans put their lives on the line to help the Iraqi people seek the light of peace. More than 4,400 Americans gave their lives, fighting for people they never knew, for values that have defined our people for more than two centuries. Tens of thousands troops were injured during battle. What their country asked of them was not small. What they sacrificed was not easy. Most painfully, since the war began, 55 members of the Fourth Stryker Brigade made the ultimate sacrifice, part of over 4,400 Americans who have given their lives in Iraq.

"I know that to my brothers in arms who fought and died, this day would probably mean a lot," a Staff Sergeant said.

I believe that God will place golden crowns on His deceased childrens' heads. He will also bless our Heroes of Foreign War.

President Obama encouraged Iraq's leaders to move forward with a sense of urgency to form an inclusive government that is just, representative, and accountable to the Iraqi people. When that government is in place, there should be no doubt that the Iraqi people will have a strong partner in the United States. Our new approach reflects a long-term partnership with Iraq, one based upon mutual interest and mutual respect. Of course, violence will not end with our combat mission. Extremists will continue to set off bombs, attack Iraqi civilians and try to spark sectarian strife. Ultimately, these terrorists will fail to achieve their goals. Iraqis are a proud people. They have rejected sectarian war, and they have no interest in endless destruction. They understand that, in the end, only Iraqis can re-solve their differences and police their streets. Only Iraqis can build a democracy within their borders. What America can do, and will do, is provide support for the Iraqi people as both a friend and a partner. Ending this war is not only in Iraq's interest, but also in ours. Vice President Biden delivered a similar message to the Iraqi people.

Old adversaries are at peace and emerging democra-cies are potential partners. New markets for our goods stretch from Asia to Americas. A new push for peace in the Middle East will begin there tomorrow. Now, that ef-fort must begin within our own borders. Sometimes in the midst of storms, trying to rebuild a lasting peace for our nation and long-term prosperity may seem beyond our reach. These milestorm should serve as a message that the future is ours to shape. It should also serve as a message that the United States of America intends to sustain and strengthen our leadership in this young century.

President Obama disagreed about the war from its outset; nevertheless, former President Bush appreciates our service men and women, and hope for Iraqis' future. The greatness of our democracy is in our ability to move beyond our differences and to learn from our experiences as we confront the many challenges ahead.

President Obama is awed at our troops sacrifice and for the sacrifices of our families. He honors our troops because they have served abroad, met every challenge, and served us faithfully. He has promised each woman and man in uniform, who donned our colors that America would do whatever it takes to serve them faithfully. We, the people, all of us, must honor and serve our veterans of foreign war with such valor. We must work together to secure the dream that many generations have fought for, including our president's grandfather: The dream that a better life awaits anyone who is willing to work and reach for it.

President Obama has already made one of the largest increases in funding for veterans in decades. We are providing the healthcare and benefits that our veterans have earned. Our doctors are treating signature war wombs that include post-traumatic stress disorder and traumatic brain injuries. The GI Bill has helped those who fought World War II, including our president's grandfather. Our ancestors were the backbone of our middle class. Our service men and women must have the chance to apply their gifts to expand the American economy because part of ending a war responsibly is standing by those who have fought it. As long as President Obama is Chief-in-Command, he will do whatever it takes to fulfill that sacred trust.

Our troop's mission ends in Iraq; nevertheless, our commitment to a sovereign, stable, and self-reliant nation continues. Under Operation New Dawn, a transitional force of U.S. troops will remain there, but with a different mission: advising and assisting Iraq's Security Forces, supporting Iraqi troops in targeted counterterrorism missions, and protecting our civilians. As our military draws down, our dedicated civilians, diplomats, aid workers, and advisors are moving into the lead to support Iraq as it strengthens its government, resolves political disputes, resettles those displaced by war, and builds ties with the region and the world. Consistent with our agreement with the Iraqi government, all U.S. troops will leave by the end of next year.

President Obama understands the ongoing security challenges we face. Throughout our history, America has been willing to bear the burden of promoting liberty and human dignity overseas, understanding its links to our own liberty and security. No challenge is more essential to our security than our fight against al Qaeda. We are now approaching our 10th year of combat in Afghanistan. Many people are understandably asking tough questions about our mission there. We must never lose sight of what is at stake. Al Qaeda continues to plot against us. Our drawdown in Iraq will enable us to apply the resources necessary for the offense. Over the last 19 months, nearly a dozen al Qaeda leaders and hundreds of al Qaeda's extremist allies have been captured or killed.

President Obama has ordered the deployment of additional troops under the command of General David Petraeus. They are fighting to break the Taliban's momentum. As with the surge in Iraq, these forces will be in place for a limited time to provide space for the Afghans to build their capacity and secure their own future. As was the case in Iraq, we cannot do for Afghans what they must ultimately do for themselves. We are currently training Afghan Security Forces and supporting a political resolution to Afghanistan's problems. Next August, our military will begin a transition to Afghan responsibility. Our troops reduction pace will be determined by the conditions on the ground, and our support for Afghanistan will endure. However, make no mistake; this transition will begin because open-ended war serves neither our interests nor the Afghan people's. Indeed, one of the lessons of our effort in Iraq is that American influence around the world is not a function of military force alone. We must use diplomacy, economic strength, and the power of America to secure our interests and stand by our allies. We must project a vision of the future based not on our fears, but our hopes: A vision that recognizes real danger existence around the world, but also the limitless possibilities of our time. As we speak, al Qaeda continues to plot against us, and its leadership remains anchored in the border regions of Afghanistan and Pakistan. We will disrupt, dismantle and defeat al Qaeda, while preventing Afghanistan from again serving as a base for terrorists. America will do more than just defeat on the battlefield those who offer hatred and destruction. We will also lead among those who are willing to work together to expand freedom and opportunity for all people. We will maintain the finest fighting force that the world has ever known. *God delivers on time.*

I believe President Obama understands this historic moment comes at a time of great uncertainty for many

Americans because of enduring a long and painful recession.

We deployed men and women in uniform to make enormous sacrifices. Our troops left much behind. Some were teenagers when the war began. The war in Iraq was a contentious issue at home. We spent vast resources abroad at a time of tight budgets at home. We have spent a trillion dollars at war, often financed by borrowing from overseas. This, in turn, has short-changed investments in our own people, and contributed to record deficits. Billions of young people want to move beyond the shackles of poverty and conflict. For too long, we have put off tough decisions on everything from our manufacturing base to our energy policy to education reform. Too many middle-class families find themselves working harder for less, while our nation's long-term competitiveness is at risk. Over the last decade, we have not done what is necessary to shore up the foundations of our own prosperity. Now, it is time to rebuild our nation, the United States of America. Our most urgent task is to restore our economy. *God delivers on time.*

Our nation is travelling through rough waters; however, President Obama and t*he 111th* Congress have addressed some issues with as much energy, grit and sense of common purpose. Congress has passed hundreds of bills that will assist us, but in a timely manner. In the meantime, we can do all things though Christ, which strengthens us. We will jumpstart industries that will create jobs and end our dependence on foreign oil. We will unleash the innovation that allows new products to roll off our assembly lines, and nurture the ideas that spring from our entrepreneurs. We will put the millions of Americans who have lost their jobs back to work. To strengthen our middle class, we will educate all of our children and give our workers the skills needed to compete in a global economy.

Operation Iraqi Freedom combat mission has ended. Our troops have completed every task given, and we will do the same. They are the steel in our ship of state. They have given us confidence that our course is true and that beyond the pre-dawn darkness, better days lie ahead. In the meantime, the Iraqi people have met their responsibility, moved into leadership with considerable skills and commitment to their fellow citizens.

Now, we must move forward with confidence and commitment. More than 3.5 million people make up our military forces, including nearly, 1.3 million active duty members, 1.1 million Reserves, and more than 800,000 Department of Defense civilian personnel. Our military families are important element to our armed forces. We nurture and support our service members during perilous times. Ask not what our military can do for us, but let us serve them by going to www.serve.org. May God bless our Heroes of a foreign war, our military families, and the United States of America. *God delivers on time.*

Conclusion:
Our Journey

Iraq, Their Mission, Our Journey, a continuation of my first publication entitled, My God Delivers On Time was written to honor our deceased mother, Evangelist/ Prophetess Sarah Mae Wilson's legacy, our Heroes of a Foreign War, which includes the Ohio Army National Guard 612th Engineer Battalion and especially the Bravo Company 1st Squad 1st Platoon (The Bad Boyz). I also dedicate this book to the families of our military.

I write books to remind us of God's Sovereignty and to invite you to become members of the body of Christ. Additionally, I write books for inspiration, motivation, and encouragement. *God delivers on time.*

God has a divine plan, purpose, and destiny for Iraq. No other nation except Israel has more biblical history and prophecy associated with it than Iraq. This nation is rich in oil supplies and other nations are trying to overtake them. Names in the Bible for Iraq are Babylon, land of Shinar, and Mesopotamia. Some biblical events that transpired in Iraq were Daniel in the lion's den, Noah building the Ark, the tower of Babel, Garden of Eden, the three Hebrew children placed in the fiery furnace, and Abraham resided there. For a better understanding of Iraq's history, read and study God's Word, using the Old Testament, and cross-reference each scripture in your Bible to verify this truth. *God delivers on time.*

Following 9-11, our troops embarked on a journey of the unknown in a foreign land. People were killing anyone representing good. A war to disarm a state became a fight against insurgency. Terrorism and sectarian warfare was tarring Iraq apart. In the meantime, our troops have made a difference. They served with courage and resolve. They completed every mission assigned. They defeated a regime that was terrorizing the Iraqi people. Our operation combat mission has ended, but our commitment to Iraq's future remains. Iraq continues to suffer terrorist attacks, but security incidents have been near the lowest on record since the war began. Iraqi forces have taken the fight to al Qaeda, removing much of its leadership in Iraqi-led operations. Iraq held credible elections that drew a strong turnout. A caretaker administration is in place as Iraqis form a government based on the results of that election. God bless our Heroes of a Foreign War.

Many of us have questioned President Bush's use of authority. Please allow me to refresh your memory. Before the creation of this world, God made us Kings and Priests unto Him.

"And hath made us Kings and Priests unto God and his Father; to him be glory and dominion for ever and ever. Amen'." Revelation 1: 6

God ordained individuals and placed them in authority. They are ministers of God, but for the good.

"1 For there is no power but of God: the powers that be are ordained of God. 2 Whosoever therefore resisteth the power resisteth the ordinance of God: and they that resist shall receive to themselves damnation. 3 For rulers are not a terror to good works, but to the evil. Wilt thou then not be afraid of the power? do that which is good, and thou shalt have praise of the same: 4 For he is the minister of God to thee for good. But if thou do that which is evil, be afraid; for he beareth not the sword in vain: for he is the minister of God, a revenger to execute wrath upon him that doeth evil. 5 Wherefore ye must needs be subject, not only for wrath, but also for conscience sake. 6 for this cause pay ye tribute also: for they are God's ministers, attending continually upon this very thing." Romans 13:1-6

God has given us the ability to choose right from wrong, and He will not condone sin. If former President Bush abused his authority, God will hold him accountable and judge his heart.

"The king's heart is in the hand of the LORD, as the rivers of water: he turneth it whithersoever he will." Proverbs 21:1 *God delivers on time.*

This season of my journey had affected me traumatically. In 2005 and 2006, Gods' angels carried Mrs. Louise (aunt) Flowers, Mr. Clyde (brother-in-law) Rogers Sr., Mrs. Martha (great aunt) Borders, Ms. Sarah (mother) Wilson, Mrs. Elizabeth (sister) Monford, Mrs. Icilda Weslenda(second mom) Halstead, and Mrs. Carolynn (sister-in-law) Wilson to the presence of God in Paradise. Their spirits also settled in our hearts. My son Todochi and godson Derek faced death while serving in Iraq. My daughter Tomika, Mikalah and I also faced death. *God delivers on time.*

God has a divine plan and purpose for America. Based on God's foreknowledge and His divine declaration, God chose the United States of America's destiny. His purpose was/is for us to fulfill His plan of salvation and be a blessing to other nations as well as our own. It is not God's will for His children to perish, but to have eternal life in Heaven with Him.

"16 For God so loved the world, that he gave his only begotten Son, that whosoever believeth in him should not perish, but have everlasting life. John 3:16

Since 9-11, "war on terror" has caused a fear-based religion that did not stand. It is essential to understand that neither wars nor tragedies can save us. We may have different paths of coming to Jesus; however, Jesus is the only way to Heaven. He is the Savior of this world. No man can come unto Jesus except those given Him by the Father and He draws us.

CONCLUSION: OUR JOURNEY

"64 But there are some of you that believe not. For Jesus knew from the beginning who they were that believed not, and who should betray him. 65 And he said, Therefore said I unto you, that no man can come unto me, except it were given unto him of my Father." John 6:64-65--"No man can come to me, except the Father which hath sent me draw him: and I will raise him up at the last day." John 6:4

Invitation to Discipleship

Is God's Spirit drawing you today? Do you believe in the death, burial, and resurrection of Jesus Christ? Do you believe Jesus died for our sins? If you believe, trust God's Word, accept His gift of salvation and by faith, you are saved. Make Jesus Christ Lord of your personal life. Welcome to the body of Christ. Be baptized as an outward testimony and sign of what God has done in your heart and testify to others.

God saved us by His grace through faith excluding boasting from all, and God would get all the glory. Our understanding of scriptures below equips us to walk in peace, joy, and freedom from Satan's condemnation.

"8 For by grace are ye saved through faith; and that not of yourselves: it is the gift of God: 9 Not of works, lest any man should boast. Ephesians 2:8-9

We all have sin and come short of God's glory; however, Jesus is faithful and just to forgive and cleanse us from all unrighteousness. When we sin, the Holy Spirit convicts us of our wrongness, so pray, repent and move forward. Do not live under or walk in condemnation.

"8 If we say that we have no sin, we deceive ourselves, and the truth is not in us. 9 If we confess our sins, he is faithful and just to forgive us our sins, and to cleanse us from all unrighteousness 10 If we say that we have not sinned, we make him a liar, and his word is not in us." John 1:8 -10

Most importantly, it is imperative that we stay with God and not turn our backs to God, becoming prodigal sons or daughters. This stage is the worse state of a person's life.

"20 For if after they have escaped the pollutions of the world through the knowledge of the Lord and Saviour Jesus Christ, they are again entangled therein, and overcome, the latter end is worse with them than the beginning. 21 righteousness, than, after they have known it, to turn from the holy commandment delivered unto them." 2 Peter 2:19-21

I thank God for choosing Jesus to atone for our sins. No sin will separate His love from us. It is crucial that we understand salvation is not a one-time experience, but an ongoing process. *God delivers on time.*

The Holy Spirit indwells us. The Holy Spirit is a marvelous gift that God has provided for us in Jesus' absence. According to *John 14:26, the* Holy Spirit is our helper and teacher. Allow Him to make a disciple of you, so you can disciple others. According to *John 16:7, the* Holy Spirit is our comforter. According to *John 16:13, the* Holy Spirit is truth, our guide, and memory. God has sealed us with the Holy Spirit of promise. He is our Heavenly Father. We are heirs, joint heirs to the Kingdom of God.

"And if children, then heirs; heirs of God, and joint-heirs with Christ; if so be that we suffer with him, that we may be also glorified together." Romans 8:17

We are no longer servants, but sons, heirs through Christ.

"6 And because ye are sons, God hath sent forth the Spirit of his Son into your hearts, crying, Abba, Father. 7 Wherefore thou art no more a servant, but a son; and if a son, then an heir of God through Christ." Galatians 4:6-7

We have an inheritance.

"13 whom ye also trusted, after that ye heard the word of truth, the gospel of your salvation: in whom also after that ye believed, ye were sealed with that holy Spirit of promise, 14 Which is the earnest of our inheritance until the redemption of the purchased possession, unto the praise of his glory." Ephesians 1:13-14

Jesus desire is to work through us by the power of the Holy Spirit. At age 12, Jesus was aware of His calling; however, He had to be empowered by the Holy Spirit. John baptized Him and a dove representing the Holy Spirit came upon Him, and He received power. Jesus ministry begins at age 30 and lasted for 3 1/2 years. He taught the Apostles about being empowered by the Holy Spirit for the work of the ministry. We need to be empowered also for the work of the ministry. God does not call the qualified. He qualifies the called.

"But ye shall receive power, after that the Holy Ghost is come upon you: and ye shall be witnesses unto me both in Jerusalem, and in all Judea, and in Samaria, and unto the uttermost part of the earth." Acts 1:8

God has given us (imperfect mortals) spiritual gifts to be helpers of one another in the constant battle against sin. His power makes the church what it is. Throughout life for every need of the soul and heart, there is a provision in the gifts of the Spirit. Discover your gift (s) in the body of Christ and be a blessing to others.

11 And he gave some, apostles; and some, prophets; and some, evangelists; and some, pastors and teachers; 12 For the perfecting of the saints, for the work of the ministry, for the edifying of the body of Christ: 13 Till we all come in the unity of the faith, and of the knowledge of the Son of God, unto a perfect man, unto the measure of the stature of the fulness of Christ: Ephesians 4:11-13   God delivers on time.

Let us be mindful that on this journey, God is not through with us yet. We have not arrived. We are not holier than Thy; however, in Christ, we are the righteousness of God. We are in right standing with Him because He died for us. In the meantime, spiritual maturity is essential for our walk in Christ. God's children are to come as is; however, we are not to remain as we came. God does not want us conformed to the things of this world, but to be transformed by the renewing of our minds.

"And be not conformed to this world: but be ye transformed by the renewing of your mind, that ye may prove what is that good, and acceptable, and perfect, will of God." Romans 12:2

God wants His children to put on the new man.

"21 If so be that ye have heard him, and have been taught by him, as the truth is in Jesus: 22 That ye put off concerning the former conversation the old man, which is corrupt according to the deceitful lusts; 23 And be renewed in the spirit of your mind; 24 And that ye put on the new man, which after God is created in righteousness and true holiness." Ephesians 1:21-24

God wants His children to produce Godly fruit; however, we must allow Him to purge from us what is not beneficial to the Kingdom. He will take some branches away and cleanse others in order to produce more fruits. We need the action of the Holy Spirit working in our lives.

"Every branch in me that beareth not fruit, he taketh away: and every branch that beareth fruit, He purgeth it, that it may bring forth more fruit." John 15: 2

God wants an intimate relationship with His children. He wants us to trust in Him, leaning not to our own understanding, but acknowledging Him in all our ways, and He will direct our path.

"5 Trust in the LORD with all thine heart; and lean not unto thine own understanding. 6 In all thy ways acknowledge him

and he shall direct thy paths." Proverbs 3:5-6

God wants, above all, for His children to prosper and be in health as our soul prospers. If we are prosperous in our soul, we can be a blessing to others.

"Beloved, I wish above all things that thou mayest prosper and be in health, even as thy soul prospereth." 3 John 1:2 God *delivers on time.*

Satan and his attacks are real. He never sleeps, slumbers, takes a break, or snoozes. He is always on his job. His ultimate goal is to devour.

"Be sober, be vigilant; because your adversary the devil, as a roaring lion, walketh about, seeking whom he may devour." 1 Peter 5:8

Satan is a deceitful lair. He is the father of all liars. He has divided our houses. God's Word declares that a house divided cannot stand.

"And Jesus knew their thoughts, and said unto them, Every kingdom divided against itself is brought to desolation: and every city or house divided against itself shall not stand." Matthews 12: 25

Satan is trying to destroy our children. They have issues. They have lost their identity. We have allowed prayer to be removed from our schools and homes. We can no longer discipline our children without legal ramification. God's Word declares that our children need training.

"6 Train up a child in the way he should go: and when he is

old, he will not depart from it." Proverbs 22:6

Our churches have issues. God's Word declares that judgment must begin at the house of the Lord.

"17 For the time is come that judgment must begin at the house of God: and if it first begin at us, what shall the end be of them that obey not the gospel of God? 18 And if the righteous scarcely be saved, where shall the ungodly and the sinner appear?" 1 Peter 4:17-18

Satan is trying to divide our nation. God's Word declares that we need to seek His face and turn from our wicket ways...

"14 If my people, which are called by my name, shall humble themselves, and pray, and seek my face, and turn from their wicked ways; then will I hear from heaven, and will forgive their sin, and will heal their land." 2 Chronicles 7:14. God delivers on time.

God's children must study God's Word, daily. All Scriptures are given by the inspiration of God and profitable for doctrine, reproof, correction and instruction in righteousness.

"16 All Scripture is given by inspiration of God, and is profitable for doctrine, for reproof, for correction, for instruction in righteousness, 17 that the man of God may be complete, thoroughly equipped for every good work." II Timothy 3: 16-17

Unbelief causes doubt to weaken our faith or cancel our faith.

"For verily I say unto you, That whosoever shall say unto

this mountain, Be thou removed, and be thou cast into the sea; and **shall** not doubt *in his* heart, but shall believe that those things which he saith shall come to pass; he shall have whatsoever he saith." Mark 11: 23   God delivers on time.*

It is vital for God's children to meditate on God's Word daily and assemble with the saints. It is also vital for us to remain prayerful. Prayer is the key to God answering our prayers. Our faith unlocks the door. We must remain steadfast, always abounding in the work of the Lord, knowing that our work is not in vain.

"Therefore, my beloved brethren, be ye stedfast, unmoveable, always abounding in the work of the Lord, forasmuch as ye know that your labour is not in vain in the Lord." 1 Corinthians 15:58

We must remain faithful to God in prayer, asking His continuous blessings for our Heroes a Foreign War, our military families, leaders, and the United States of America. We must pray for God's chosen nation, Israel, and other nations. We must pray for our enemies. We must never forget to pray for ourselves. Most of all, we must give God the praise, honor, and glory for who He is, what He is doing, and going to manifest in our lives. *God delivers on time.*

A Tribute to
Mother Sarah Mae Wilson

God's Gift

Mother Sarah Wilson was God's gift to Samuel, Inez, Isaiah, Boyd, Raymond, and I. She was also our sister in Christ and best friend. Her sacrifices spoke louder than words. She loved, encouraged, shared, fasted and prayed, showed concern, disciplined, chastised, and supported our efforts for the Kingdom of God. She was God's gift to us. We loved her, will always love her, but God loved her best. This tribute is from the Wilson's family.

My God Delivers On Time

The Wilson's Family
(2003)

Jackie, Mother, and Inez
Isaiah, Samuel, and Raymond

Mother Sarah Wilson and Aunt Louise Flowers (2003)

Mother Wilson "80" Birthday Celebration Group Picture (2003)

Mother Wilson and Sons
Samuel, Isaiah, and Raymond
(2003)

Mother Wilson and Daughters
Jackie and Inez
(2003)

Mother Wilson and Granddaughters
Keesha and Tomika
(2005)

Mother Wilson and Great-Granddaughters
Diamond, Amarous, SaKeyna, and TaQuayla
(2003)

Mother Wilson and Great-grandsons
Kevin, Marquis, and Camrin
(2005)

Mother Wilson's last-Great-grandchild
Mikalah (2005)

Mother Wilson's Neice
Reather H. Chambers

Mother Wilson's STNA
Jenera Knuckles

Mother's 81st B-Day and Jackie (2004)

Mother's 82nd B-Day and Jackie (2005)

Mother Wilson (1988)

Mother Wilson (1947)

Mother Wilson's Great- great-grandson Derrick and Great -grandson Johnavin (Jackie's great- grand son and grandson)

Jackie's granddaughter, Gabrielle Mae

Jackie's granddaughter Chardenay and Johnavin

Mother Wilson and Jackie's Last Easter Dinner (2005)

Evangelist/Prophetess Sarah Mae Wilson
Our Mother's Last Ministering Picture
(2005)

My God Delivers On Time

A FRIENDSHIP THAT WILL NEVER BREAK

Thank you for the laughter,
The good times that we shared.
Thank you for always listening,
For trying to be fair.

Thank you for your comfort,
When things were going bad.
Thank you for your shoulder to cry on,
When I was sad.

This gift is a reminder,
That all of my lifetime through.
I will be thanking Heaven for,
A special friend like you.

From Mother Wilson
To Jackie

My God Delivers On Time

About the Authoress

Jackie Ruth Wilson was born to Mr. & Mrs. Clarence and Sarah Wilson in Lawndale, North Carolina on July 4, 1952. She has four brothers and one sister. The late Rev. Herbert and Mrs. Amanda Littlejohn Borders, her grandparents, reared her during Mother Wilson's employment. Her grandparents, parents, one brother and a sister are deceased.

Jackie gave her life to Christ at a young age. She married at age 21. God blessed her with three children including Keesha, Tomika, and Todochi. Following her 16 years of marriage, she divorced. Heartbroken and devastated, she became an addict and alcoholic for seven years and was dying without hope of recovery.

From the time of her birth, God was laying the foundation for her to write, My God Delivers On Time. You can purchase her book at www.createspace.com/3107362

Read her story and be blessed.

Jackie continues her story in this book entitled, Iraq, Their Mission, Our Journey, through the deployment of her son to Iraq, the bereavement of her Mother and other family deaths, births, many healings, deliverance, and spiritual growth. She is no longer fighting the God given mantle passed to her by her Mother. Every trial set before her taught her to give thanks and glorify God in all things.

Jackie is a graduate of Thomson High School in Scranton, PA. She attended Ohio State Beauty Academy. She graduated from Penn Foster Career School, receiving a Medical Coding and Billing Career Certificate. She was a member of the American Academy of Professional Coders. She received a diploma from, the Voice of Prophecy Correspondence School and a certificate of completion from, Herbert W. Armstrong Bible Correspondence School. She is a member of Organizing For America, a project of the Democratic National Committee. Her e-mail addresses are jrw1952@ gmail and wilson.jackie5953@yahoo.com. You can purchase her book at www.outskirtspress.com/iraqtheirmissionourjourney. You can purchase her first publication entitled, My God Delivers On Time at www.createspace.com/3107362. You can also purchase her designs at www.cafepress.com/jrwdesigns. You may follow Ms Wilson on the World Wide Web: www.facebook.com;www.myspace.com;www.blackplanet.com; www.twitter.com.

The authoress currently peacefully resides in Lima, Ohio. Still in the midst of going through battles, she enjoys being an evangelist, mother, grandmother, great-grandmother, designer, and whatever else God needs for her to be.

My God Delivers On Time